AF731632

SUCCESSFUL BUSINESS PLANS

JANE KHEDAIR AND MICHAEL ANDERSON

Viva Books

New Delhi | Mumbai | Chennai | Kolkata | Bangalore | Hyderabad | Kochi | Guwahati

Copyright © Business Plans Services Ltd.

First Indian Edition 2010

VIVA BOOKS PRIVATE LIMITED

- 4737/23 Ansari Road, Daryaganj, New Delhi 110 002
  E-mail: vivadelhi@vivagroupindia.net, Tel. 42242200
- 76, Service Industries, Shirvane, Sector 1, Nerul, Navi Mumbai 400 706
  E-mail: vivamumbai@vivagroupindia.net, Tel. 27721273, 27721274
- Jamals Fazal Chambers, 26 Greams Road, Chennai 600 006
  E-mail: vivachennai@vivagroupindia.net, Tel. 28290304, 28294241
- B-103, Jindal Towers, 21/1A/3 Darga Road, Kolkata 700 017
  E-mail: vivakolkata@vivagroupindia.net, Tel. 22836381, 22816713
- 7, Sovereign Park Apartments, 56-58, K. R. Road, Basavanagudi, Bangalore 560 004
  E-mail: vivabangalore@vivagroupindia.net, Tel. 26607409, 26607410
- 101-102 Mughal Marc Apartments, 3-4-637 to 641, Narayanguda, Hyderabad 500 029
  E-mail: vivahyderabad@vivagroupindia.net, Tel. 27564481, 27564482
- Beevi Towers, First Floor, SRM Road, Kaloor, Kochi 682 018, Kerala
  E-mail: vivakochi@vivagroupindia.net, Tel: 0484-2403055, 2403056
- 232, GNB Road, Beside UCO Bank, Silpukhuri, Guwahati 781 003
  E-mail: vivaguwahati@vivagroupindia.net, Tel: 0361-2666386

www.vivagroupindia.com

Published by arrangement with

Crimson Publishing,
a division of Crimson Business Ltd
Westminster House, Kew Road
Richmond, Surrey TW9 2ND

All rights reserved. No part of this book may be reproduced or utilized in any form or by any means, electronic or mechanical, including photocopying, recording or by any information storage or retrieval systems, without permission in writing from the publisher.

This edition is for sale in the Indian subcontinent only. Not for export elsewhere.

ISBN : 978-81-309-1497-8

Published by Vinod Vasishtha for Viva Books Private Limited, 4737/23, Ansari Road, Daryaganj, New Delhi - 110 002.

Printed and bound by Raj Press, R-3, Inderpuri, New Delhi - 110 012.

CONTENTS

ACKNOWLEDGEMENTS

We would like to acknowledge the helpful influence on our work of material originally conceived at London Business School.

In particular, we appreciate the input past and present by The Foundation for Entrepreneurial Management in general, and in particular the work of John Bates, Michael Hay, John Mullins and Maurice Pinto. Anything in this book which benefits from work they have done is gratefully appreciated. Any errors or distortions of such material are our responsibility.

We are also grateful to Derek Anderson CBE and Dr Armad D'Augar for the inspiration they provided for the cartoons in this book.

Jane Khedair
Michael Anderson

PREFACE

Jane Khedair

I sat on the adversarial side of a City analyst's desk throughout the 1990s, and it came as no surprise to those who knew me that a move away from the daily drudge of the corporate world to one of running my own business represented a more appealing option. What better way of making use of invaluable first-hand experience of evaluating, scoring and re-writing business plans than to establish a dedicated support service for people wishing to start, grow or rescue a business? Better this than to allow budding entrepreneurs like you to continue like lambs to the slaughter, facing negativity and rejection at each iteration of your business plan as you approach and are eliminated by yet another audience.

Some 17 years later and indebted to the support that I have enjoyed from both London Business School and my fellow directors, I am delighted and excited to have been invited to share our wisdom, knowledge and experience – good and bad – with you. I hope you are able to learn as much as we have, albeit somewhat more speedily, to ensure that your business plan secures you a fast-track route to success without too many painful and expensive lessons along the way.

Take your family, friends and only those who you wholly trust along a business plan journey that you can be sure you'll never forget.

Michael Anderson

After trading commodities and financial futures in the City for 5 years, I bought a specialist printing business and ran it for 12 years before selling up and spending a year at London Business School on the Sloan Masters programme – the theory following the practice as some might say. A year later I became Chief Executive of a cutting edge e-learning business, which raised over £3 million of venture capital, and subsequently became a Director of Business Plan Services Ltd. BPS is the definitive resource for business planning in the UK, seeing hundreds of business plans each year and helping entrepreneurs to improve them.

During all this activity, I started to dip my toe in the water as a business angel, i.e. someone who invests money for a minority share in other people's businesses. It has been my great good fortune in angel investment to have defied the miserable statistics and make a reasonable return on time and money spent. There have been ups and downs, the downs generally coming for extended periods before the ups. In this book, I have tried to capture the key points which have contributed to the success I have been fortunate enough to enjoy. It is my hope that reading this book will provide you with a short-cut to emulating that success, in part by enabling you to write the perfect business plan.

I have learned to accept the fact that it is especially rare for any business plan to reflect reality even 6-12 months after it has been written. We cannot foresee the future. The most we can hope for is that the underlying purpose, the vision for the business, remains the same even if the smart entrepreneur is flexible enough to adapt to changing circumstances. My most successful investments have been as a result of meeting outstanding entrepreneurs with a clear vision, and I intend to demonstrate in this book that a great business plan can build on that starting point.

Over the last 23 years, I have looked at businesses and business plans as an entrepreneur, as a manager, as an academic and as an investor. With the benefit of this unusual perspective, I have come to understand that anyone can write a business plan but that there is a knack to writing a successful one, which grabs the reader's attention and adds value to the business; equally, there are many pitfalls in business plan writing, which lead to the reader losing interest very quickly. In this book I have tried to marry the needs of the business plan writer and the business plan reader whatever the objective of the plan may be. Most often this is raising finance, but it is not necessarily so.

I have been delivering a regular monthly workshop at The British Library to help guide entrepreneurs in the art – for it certainly is an art rather than a science – of how to write a business plan. The wonder which greets me from so many in the audience makes me think that perhaps this is more of a dark art than I thought.

I make no pretence that this book can cover all types of business plan. Specific business concerns need to be addressed differently, but my hope is that this book addresses the individuality of the audience as widely as possible whilst remaining generic in its nature. For those who feel that their issues have not been met, Business Plan Services would be happy to hear from you why your business is so different from the norm. My intention is to address a broad spectrum of entrepreneurs, who are mesmerised by the excess of advice on business plans and who seek only a simple layman's guide to the principles of business plan writing.

Before her untimely death Dame Anita Roddick of Body Shop fame wrote an article entitled *"Don't get a business degree, get angry"* and posted it on the British Library website under the title *"Why I'm glad I never went to business school"*. She was, of course, right that so much that is good and necessary in entrepreneurialism comes in the category of inspiration and determination, but this book is designed to demonstrate that discipline and planning grafted onto raw passion give an entrepreneur an even greater chance of success.

We live in uncertain times, and the pace of change is likely to keep accelerating regardless of whether the wider economy improves or declines. I have tried to set out some guidelines and rules to help the budding entrepreneur to steer a path to success whatever the economic conditions may be.

Good luck.

CHAPTER 1

The purpose of a business plan

This chapter looks at what a business plan is and why you need one. It also looks at the different audiences for a business plan and how this affects what you need to include. Finally, it touches on the need for passion in your business plan, to make your readers as excited as you are.

WHAT IS A BUSINESS PLAN?

A common definition of a business plan describes it as: an explanation of business goals, why you think you can achieve these goals, and how you plan to reach them. This is a fairly general statement and covers many elements, which range from sketchy outline ideas that are mapped out on the back of an envelope to a lengthy encyclopaedia of a document that nobody ever has enough time or inclination to read.

What makes a business plan useful?

We have looked at literally hundreds if not thousands of business plans over the years, written by people looking to start or grow their own business. What is clear is that there is no such thing as a standard business plan. However, in essence they should all cover the same ground and, as set out in any good business plan guide, will feature a consistent set of chapter or section headings, not least because these will be familiar to your audience. These will set out what the business is aiming to sell, who to, and where and how its customers can be found and reached. It will also cover who else is trying to sell to them, what resource (typically money and people) you will need and how much profit the business can ultimately make from its trading activities over the next three years.

As straightforward as these topics sound, it is the strength of the underlying content that sets one business plan apart from another. Strong content will enable it to be used as a viable business plan that is ready for execution. If the content is not useful enough, the business plan will become merely a collection of unjustified, ill-thought-through statements that lack any weight or substance and so represent nothing more than a plan of ideas rather than action.

A good business plan is a document written using researched statements to give weight to all aspects of an entrepreneur's aspirations for his business, enabling those ideas to become reality.

The business plan is therefore a means to an end – a platform for the management or owner, which forces them to think through all the relevant aspects of their business. Whilst the business plan alone cannot secure success for the business, we can confidently endorse the over-used maxim that 'failing to plan is planning to fail'.

WHY DO YOU NEED A BUSINESS PLAN?

The first question from a potential client is frequently: 'Can you write a business plan for me?' and we always answer: 'Why do you need one?' and 'Who is going to read it?' Without the answers to these questions, it is impossible to write an appropriate plan. A plan that takes no account of its audience will be a waste of effort. Business success does not depend on the existence of a plan, but the lack of one will make failure more likely.

TOP TIPS

Working out what your business plan is for is the first step to creating a useful business plan.

The purpose of your business plan

First of all then, you need to assess what a business plan will do for you. Do you think that it will help you get your business to where you want it to be, or do you anticipate that preparing a business plan will be a time wasting exercise, which is nothing but a distraction from your day-to-day tasks? 'Haven't I got enough to do?' you may ask yourself. We are all busier now than ever, but remember: being busy and being productive are two very different things.

Many business owners spend their day running round in circles, fighting fires, without any idea about what they should be doing in order to make a difference to their business. Having a well thought-through business plan, which sets out your vision and goals for the business, will force you to work out how to reach the point you want to get to. Ideally, you will also have included an action plan with attainable timeframes that tells you what you should be doing and when.

By writing a useful business plan, *you* will be in control of your business rather than *it* being in control of you!

You will have identified what you need to do in an orderly and structured way in order to get your business to the next stage of its life. Without a business plan you risk finding yourself responding to situations that arise in the business or in the market, instead of leading the business forward as a focused entrepreneur.

ACTION POINT

Work out who will read your business plan and what the purpose of your business plan is for your particular business.

QUESTIONS YOU NEED TO CONSIDER

OK, so you can now see the benefit of providing a focused road map for your business and you have taken on board the fact that you need a business plan – after all, your bank has been asking you for one for the past three months! Whilst the hours that you need to spend drafting it may feel wasted, rest assured you will benefit from actually taking time out from the day-to-day operations to think about your business. No matter how much you may resent the time you spend locked away thinking through the various components of your business plan, it is a golden opportunity to take a step back from your business and consider it impartially.

So, perhaps for the first time, you need to reason with yourself about what you want from your business and how you are going to get there. Although you may already know that you are going to make widgets for the next 'must-have' mobile phone, have you thought about who your customer is? Is it the mobile phone user or perhaps the mobile phone manufacturer? Why would they buy what you are offering? Are they likely to buy it from you when there are other people trying to sell them the same type of product? It is only when you take time out to identify who else is trying to sell to your target customers, and at what price, that you start to be able to work out how you can differentiate your business rather than just keep on banging the same drum that you would have done without having gone through the business plan exercise.

Hopefully, the benefits of having the plan are gradually becoming clearer and you are beginning to realise that this work of art that you are starting to create may well have some use after all…working out what you didn't know you didn't know! Throughout the rest of this book we will guide you through the mechanics of answering these questions, so that your business plan becomes an essential tool for your business.

WHY TEMPLATES ARE NOT ENOUGH

Many people mistakenly believe that there is a standard format and tone for a business plan. Sample business plans can be sourced easily enough and are often personalised only by changing the name of the business and its location, in anticipation that one size fits all. This trend has grown with the increased availability of free templates, which are in reality no better than a spreadsheet which provides formulae but no substance or answers. The style, substance and tone of a business plan are at least as important as the generally recognised template format.

Content needs to be tailored to your needs and only tools relevant to your business should be used. Unfortunately, meaningless mission statements and irrelevant SWOT (Strengths, Weaknesses, Opportunities and Threats) analyses are still prevalent and often gratuitously inserted by a writer to be able to tick a box in the document's contents. Of course, a mission statement may well give a reader a general view of where the business is heading, and a Five Forces diagram (which used to be a key but overused component of market analysis) built into an overall analysis of the competitive pressures on your business could be useful in some circumstances. Similarly a SWOT analysis, as an integral part of your discussion about how you recognise and intend to meet the challenges your business faces, will be helpful. (See chapter 11 for more on SWOT analysis.) However, it is the use of these tools by themselves, based on templates found in generic business plan books or software, that weaken rather than strengthen the overall plan.

TOP TIPS

Your business plan must be tailored to the needs of your business and the questions your audience will have – one size does not fit all!

A successful business plan presents a story and, just like any story, must have a flow to it, a traditional beginning, middle and end. Each section of the plan must reflect the other sections rather than there being a collection of isolated statements. It should present a picture that is comprehensive and comprehensible, the purpose and ambition being clear at every stage, drawing conclusions from each set of statements to give the document credibility and focus.

WHO IS THE AUDIENCE?

So, when writing a plan you need to start by working out who it is for. There are many reasons for writing a plan, and each one requires a different approach. For example:

- Getting a loan from a bank.
- Raising money from a business angel or venture capital investor.
- As a strategic road map for the business to provide an action plan for management which they can share with everyone else in the business.
- As a year-end plan for the boss to show where the business is heading.
- As an aid to selling the business.

Each of these audiences is seeking different information from the plan, and so it would be absurd – and unproductive – for them all to be written in the same way. Let's take a look at the different kinds of information you should include for your intended audience.

ACTION POINT

Having identified who will read your business plan earlier, you now need to research the needs of that audience – what are their key requirements and how can you meet these with your business?

Business plans for a bank manager

The bank manager wants to see two key answers in the plan, quite apart from a sound business proposition and credible management:

- Security for the debt, ie how and when is the capital going to be repaid.
- Evidence of the business' ability to service the debt by paying interest.

The business plan must focus, therefore, on how the business will meet these two needs. (Both of these key answers will be covered in more detail later in chapters 4 and 9).

In an early-stage business these two requirements are usually hard to demonstrate. Very few early-stage businesses generate cash quickly. Very few start-up entrepreneurs are fortunate enough to have access to security for the debt they seek. If the debt is required for fixed assets, eg capital equipment for manufacturing, there may be sufficient security in the equipment alone. For those who are seeking debt for day-to-day working capital, eg to finance customers' extended payments and general costs, but have no security, the Enterprise Finance Guarantee (EFG) may be ideal. Details of this scheme can be found at the Department for Business, Enterprise and Regulatory Reform (BERR) website: http://www.berr.gov.uk. See more detail in chapter 10 under *Sources of Finance*. The EFG has replaced and extended the Small Firms Loan Guarantee Scheme (SFLG), one of the most successful and valuable support programmes for early-stage businesses in the UK.

A busy bank manager will want to be presented with a snapshot of the business and its management team to assess quickly whether the rest of the document should be given more of his valuable time. Below is an extract from a sample business plan that clearly sets out the strength of the proposition, reflected in the business' solid financial performance, and the long-standing experience of the team, providing the ideal backdrop to attract the reader's attention.

EXAMPLE

Sample Executive Summary

Mr Smith-Harris owns and operates a successful shop in central London, known as The Snackbox, selling gourmet soups and salads to local workers at lunchtime. Due to the success of the first store Mr Smith-Harris is currently planning to expand into five additional London locations, targeting the same market segment.

Mr Smith-Harris opened his first store in December 2001. Since then the business' management has built a profitable company with a loyal following and powerful brand identity. The store is currently showing annual revenues of nearly £450,000.

The store is supplied from its satellite kitchen in Euston. The kitchen has the capacity to also supply several new stores from its current set up.

One of the main advantages of The Snackbox is its product offering, soups and salads, which are sold in different seasons, allowing the business to be profitable year round.

The business is owned by a UK registered company (The Snackbox Ltd) which is 80% owned and managed by Paul Smith-Harris. It started trading in December 2001. Mr Smith-Harris has many years of experience in the catering sector. At The Snackbox he is responsible for the day-to-day running of the company, marketing, public relations and new business development. He is also involved in product development. He is supported by shop and kitchen staff and will employ an admin person once the new stores open.

The Snackbox's market is a very attractive one. Key Note estimates that the size of the UK Fast Food and Home Delivery market was £8.2bn in 2008, up from £6.55bn in 2007. This represents a growth of 25.1%. Key Note forecasts the market will grow from £8.2bn in 2009 to £9.4bn in 2011. This represents a growth of 14.3%.

The Snackbox is a highly profitable business. The company will generate a small loss after tax of –£1,717 in the year ending 31 May 2009, a profit of £152,724 in the year ending 31 May 2010, £477,574 in the year ending 31 May 2011 and £600,978 in the year ending 31 May 2012.

Management assumes that it will open five new shops in total, in:
- *January 2010*
- *June 2010*
- *November 2010*
- *April 2011*
- *September 2011*

For each new shop management assumes rental deposit and refurbishment costs of £110,000.

The business is premised on a proven successful model that is cash generative and profitable. It is looking to raise £200,000 to finance the first of these two store openings and has strong cash flows to be able to service bank funding (capital and interest repayments) as well as finance all other store openings from its increased turnover at that time. Any shortfall in security should be available under the terms of the Small Firms Loan Guarantee Scheme.

This extract comes from a business plan which was successful in raising bank finance. It clearly addresses the requirements of the bank in the following ways:

- Showing that the business has a trading history.
- Clearly identifying the business' activity and how it generates cash.
- Highlighting the efficient operation of the centralised business to demonstrate its ability to generate increased turnover from an increased number of locations.
- Refering to the experience of the management to establish credibility.
- Giving headline forecast financials that demonstrate the business' potential.
- Summarising the growth trends in the market to justify its stability.
- Describing a clear expansion plan with relevant and realistic timescales.
- Identifying an exact funding requirement.
- Refering to the availability of security.

Whatever the situation, a business plan seeking debt which does not address the bank's two fundamental issues (availability of security and how the debt will be serviced) will be of no value. Both issues should be clearly addressed in the financial narrative section of the business plan, which we will look at in detail later in chapter 10.

Business plans for investment capital

Angel or venture capital investors have a very different point of view from bankers. Unlike lenders, who are looking to get their money back, plus interest, angel investors are seeking explosive returns on capital – high risk for which inflated reward is demanded. Dividends are unusual in an early-stage business, and realisation of capital, ie return of investors' money, generally comes only at exit via share sale. The expected returns may vary from 20% pa for a mature business to 60%+ pa for a start-up. Since this book is largely focused on early-stage SMEs (small and medium-sized enterprises), we can assume that the returns required are nearly 60% pa. A 60% compound growth over a five year period can be broken down as follows:

Sample compound growth table to illustrate investor returns

Period	Capital Valuation	Annual Growth Rate	Annual Growth in Capital	Total Valuation
Year 1	£100,000	60%	£60,000	£160,000
Year 2	£160,000	60%	£96,000	£256,000
Year 3	£256,000	60%	£153,600	£409,600
Year 4	£409,600	60%	£245,760	£655,360
Year 5	£655,360	60%	£393,216	£1,048,576

So, if an investor puts £100,000 into a business in Year 1, he will expect that sum of money to be worth just over £1,000,000 when he gets paid out for his share of the business in five years' time. The £100,000 will have been expected to have grown incrementally as shown above, based on the valuation of the company in accordance with its performance as each year passes.

You may be surprised that a 60% annual growth rate equates to approximately 10 times return on an investor's money over a five year period. However, this scale of appreciation comes as no surprise to angels who so frequently lose their investment. An angel investor is looking to identify growth in sales without a corresponding rise in costs (known as scalability), as this is essential to achieving the explosive growth which is the goal of an investor. If you understand this crucial point about an investor's mindset and translate it into visible scalability in your business plan, you will have gone a long way towards making an investment in your business look attractive to a potential investor.

So it quickly becomes clear that a business which is, at best, only able to generate an attractive lifestyle for the entrepreneur or the business' management team, is of limited appeal to an investor, who is looking for domination in a field that will be able to generate high growth returns for everyone. It is easy on paper to compare the potential of a retail concept whose brand and systems are capable of being rolled out across multiple locations with an independently owned shop that just about makes its owner a living. Realistically, however, very few businesses are able to aspire to these growth criteria, and entrepreneurs become disappointed that they cannot raise external finance for them. All too many business plans seeking investment lack the necessary global ambition, and the potential for growth without spiralling costs, to provide the required returns. The inappropriate use of so-called J-Curve or hockey stick financial projections, where an unrealistic growth rate of sales is graphically depicted to appease the hopes and aspirations of investors, is dealt with further in chapter 10.

This aspect of finding the best return on capital (ideally with the least risk) is a crucial and often absent theme in business plans, whether they are for start-ups or mature businesses. For this reason, it is not possible to write *the* definitive business plan for any business. Business plans are about making choices –

choices of where to allocate scarce capital. That is why writing a well-crafted plan takes time and thought and input from all of the management team.

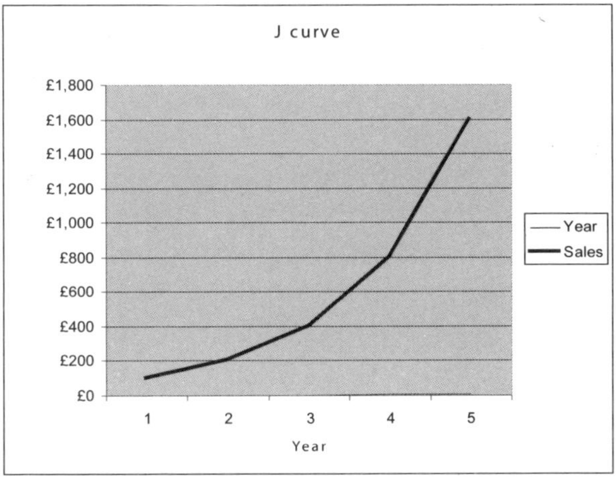

Typical J-Curve or 'hockey-stick' sales graph

ACTION POINT

Try to be realistic about the potential of your business and what you want/ expect from it. Are you offering something so unique that it has the potential to carve out a unique place and enjoy growth nationally or even internationally? Or does your business have appeal to only a limited local audience even if it may well be able to support you in a lifestyle which you would be happy with over the next few years? Answering these questions will affect who you approach for funding and how you target your business plan.

Internal business plans

An internal business plan written for the company's management is quite different from either of the first two categories which have been written for the purpose of attracting finance. In contrast, an internal business plan is typically the result of a brainstorming session whereby all members of the team have agreed on a way forward for the business. The internal plan crystallises this thought process in a document that can be shared among the whole company. The reasons for creating an internal plan are wide ranging: perhaps the management team is documenting their strategy for the future, justifying budget allocation, providing evidence of job security and a career path, presenting a clear roadmap and an understanding of any innovation that is to be used.

Internal business plans for larger organisations tend to be departmental plans, and so you need to address the financial objectives of the organisation. In particular, senior management will want to understand why resources should be allocated to your department instead of any other department; indeed why your department should not be outsourced or re-structured completely. Above all, the internal business plan and the process that is typically undertaken to arrive at this point provide the opportunity to align everyone's thoughts. Aside from quickly identifying who's who in your team it will also highlight any gaps that may well have otherwise been concealed from being too close to the day-to-day operation of the business.

EXAMPLE

Internal business planning provides the opportunity to evaluate what aspects of a business are working properly and those which would benefit from a new way of working or perhaps from a complete overhaul. Sometimes internal changes are needed as a result of external (or market) influences, as was identified by Company X, one of the UK's leading educational consultancies. Company X wanted to develop a three year business plan as an internal roadmap to evaluate opportunities from the three areas within which the client company was operating:

i) Content Development
ii) Research
iii) Training

Of these, Research was regarded as the fastest growing field and generated a 90% margin, whereas Content Development generated the largest proportion of the company's turnover but was an unpredictable source of revenue because it was wholly project driven.

The client company then enjoyed a gross income of £2m pa which they aimed to grow to approximately £3.5m within the next two to three years, potentially broken down as follows:

- *Content Development: to be sustained at approx £1m pa*
- *Research: to grow from £750,000 to £2m pa*
- *Training: to grow from £150,000 to £500,000 pa*

The client's market included blue chip companies, charities and, in the main, public sector organisations.

The client's management undertook an in-depth business planning process to deliver a new three year business plan that would provide direction for the company, its management team and staff, to determine where and how the company should focus its efforts.

The interaction from and 'buy in' of everyone concerned was regarded as integral to the effective implementation of the company's future strategy.

Business plans to sell a business

Most readers of this book are probably just thinking about starting or are in the early days of running a new business, so the idea of selling your business seems a long way off. However, a fourth reason for writing a business plan is to show clearly why someone should buy the business from you. By the time you are ready to sell the business, the planning skills and discipline you will have acquired throughout the life of your business will certainly stand you in good stead. At this stage, the structure and format will remain pretty much the same, but you will be faced with the challenge of convincing your reader that the business represents a great opportunity whilst at the same time addressing the inevitable question about why you want to sell it if it has such enormous potential.

Clearly, then, one of the main questions that you will need to answer in this kind of business plan is to spell out your reasons for wanting to sell it – however personal they may be! In fact, the more personal the better as this will demonstrate that your decision is in no way related to the business and ensure that it remains appealing to a prospective purchaser.

Passion and vision

Above all use your business plan as an opportunity to showcase the passion and vision you have for your business. Try to get others as excited as you are.

Now that we have covered the different types of audience for a business plan, and why it is so important to tailor it for each purpose, we will move on to how to make sure your business idea is strong enough to stand up to scrutiny.

QUICK RECAP

- *Work out why you are writing the business plan – is it for the management team or do you need to raise finance?*
- *If you are looking to raise finance decide on the potential of your business and its immediate capacity to generate cash to help you understand the best route for your business.*
- *Determine what different audiences will want to read about.*
  - *Are they a bank that is concerned about security and cash flow?*
  - *Are they investors who will want explosive growth in the value of their shares and a clearly identifiable way for them to get their money out of your business in three to five years time?*
  - *Are they existing or future members of the company who you will want to be inspired to work with and for you?*
  - *Are they interested in buying the business, and so will want to know why you are selling it?*
- *Work out how you are going to demonstrate that your business can meet their needs.*
- *Identify your audience – do you have more than one audience type?*
- *Amend your initial business plan to suit the needs of an additional audience.*
- *Show your passion to inspire the readers of your business plan with your vision.*

CHAPTER 2

Testing your idea

One of the most common errors in writing a plan is lack of preparation. Sitting down to write a business plan without understanding the essential background and doing some homework can be a big mistake. In this chapter we will take you through the key ways to test your idea is ready, including the key tests of whether you have a good idea or whether you have a real entrepreneurial commercial opportunity.

MIRROR, SIGNAL... *BEFORE* YOU MANOEUVRE!

Too many people start businesses by jumping in at the deep end and then realise that it is too late only when they have everything on the line. Similarly, too few people in existing businesses have tested their plans to grow their business before committing their thoughts to paper. We have all had great ideas – in the bath, over a few glasses of wine, sitting in traffic – but how many of those have been turned into a business or at least are potentially capable of being so? What makes your idea unique? Is there something innovative about your business that makes it different and, if so, how can that point of distinction be seen as something that its user – your potential customer – will value? We will see later how important it is to demonstrate both innovation and value when trying to launch a new business.

Do not forget that ideas are cheap whereas successful businesses cost, and hopefully make, money.

TOP TIPS

John Mullins' book *The New Business Road Test* is recommended as a starting point on what you should do before you write your business plan, providing the perfect opportunity to undertake some all important homework before you go any further.

So, you have done some reading and shared your business idea with a few close friends and family to get you more excited than ever that your idea really is *the* next big thing. Before going any further, we suggest that you go through a seven-point checklist to make sure that your 'idea' already has what it takes to become, or can be developed into, a money-making business. Rise to the challenge and take comfort in the fact that it is rare for any idea to pass all the tests with flying colours straight away. By identifying and addressing weaknesses now, your business plan will be stronger to cope with what is to come.

THE SEVEN TESTS OF AN ENTREPRENEURIAL OPPORTUNITY

The rocky road ahead will certainly be made much smoother if you can answer 'yes' to each and every one of the following:

1. Does the opportunity match your experience, skills and interests?

Ask yourself whether your business opportunity matches not just your interests but also your experience and skills. All too often, we are approached by keen people who have had glittering careers in investment banks or large corporations, waving a business plan that claims to offer the next big thing in food retailing or consumer technology; but surely the skills needed to run an entrepreneurial business are significantly different from those needed in either financial engineering or a large corporation? Successful entrepreneurial businesses are often built on gut feeling and risk taking, both of which are often discouraged by employers in large organisations.

However, regardless of your background, there can be no better way of identifying a gap in the market and a business opportunity than by drawing on personal experience as a result of having not been able to find a solution to your own problem…just make sure that there are enough people who share your taste and preferences.

Are you the right person?

Once you are satisfied that a market opportunity exists, the next question to ask yourself is what makes this opportunity *yours* as opposed to anyone else's. In other words what makes *you* the right person to seize this chance when there may be many others in your position looking for that 'next big thing'? We will explore differentiation in chapter 4 when we look at product, but it is important to raise this issue even at this early stage, since the lack of it can be a real potential barrier to growth. Too many people get stuck in 'me-too' businesses where the only competitive edge is price. There is no future in such a business unless you are able to produce your product at a much lower cost than your competitors, otherwise they will simply undercut you for as long as they can afford to do so.

The answer to this challenge must be innovation, ie being different, whether through creating new products or services (even at the expense of cannibalising – replacing – your own existing products and services), or as a result of improved efficiency by introducing new processes. These are the potential keys to building businesses, and they remain at the core of this book.

TOP TIPS

Bear in mind that the majority of Hewlett- Packard's revenues come from products that did not exist a year ago.

So, what is it that makes you uniquely well placed to exploit this opportunity? Identifying the answer to this can unlock one of the answers to how the plan may best be written. You may have a unique understanding of a market or you may have a unique background, which means that you can respond to an unmet need in the market. Either way, something about *you* must set your business aside from anyone else's.

2. Can you recruit and lead the team needed to exploit the opportunity that you have identified?

Look at the areas in which you are lacking. What about operational expertise? Even if you can outsource financial and marketing expertise, there still needs to be an internal understanding of how cash flow can dramatically affect a business. Equally, very few (if any) businesses can survive without marketing what they do in some guise or another. Of course, not all entrepreneurs have a handle on all these functions, especially if they have worked purely in line management positions previously. Where this type of day-to-day expertise is missing, it is vital to have others in the management team who recognise their importance and can identify how to plug any gaps. It is all very well understanding the sector you are going to be working in but not if you don't know how to make money from it.

Once you have assembled your team, you will need to consider your ability to manage the team. If you are that would-be entrepreneur and visionary individual who may not have the talent to recruit and lead such a team, it is important that you recognise your shortcomings and bring a partner into the business who does have people skills.

Recent research has identified the ideal members of an entrepreneurial management team as having:

- Proven, relevant experience in the industry, market or technology.
- A track record in achieving results, particularly profit and loss account responsibility.
- Diversity of personal qualities, styles and perspectives.
- Completeness and balance in terms of skills and expertise.
- Mutual trust, commitment and ability to manage conflict.

It may come as a surprise to learn that the greatest influence on angel investors in making their investment decision is the quality of the management team. Most of the successful entrepreneurial companies have been characterised by the strength of their personnel. Cobra Beer is one of our favourite examples, a company with which one of the authors of this book has been connected since its earliest days. It is an excellent example of much that is great in our entrepreneurial culture. Above all, the personnel at Cobra form a long-standing, cohesive and balanced team led by a visionary leader in Karan, now Lord, Bilimoria. Not only has he been a great leader in his own right but also he took an even more unusual step of standing aside to be Chairman and recruiting a professional Managing Director. This may prove to be easier said than done successfully.

While it can sometimes be lonely being an entrepreneur, you should never have to look too far for help if your opportunity is truly a money making idea. 'Where will I find these partners and managers?' is the frequent cry from frustrated entrepreneurs. The answer is that the best port of call is typically your own networks. You know a group of people. They will each know a group of like-minded people. If you can specify your requirements clearly enough it is highly likely that someone can be identified from within your network or even your network's network to fill the role.

3. What resources have you got that others are missing?

The key resources in a successful business, apart from people, are:

- Intellectual Property ('know-how'), which can sometimes be protected by patents.
- Property, especially prime locations for retail businesses.
- Capital equipment such as machinery.
- Facilities.
- Materials.
- Customer and supplier relationships.

If your unique resource is Intellectual Property, take care to protect it by taking specialist advice from a patent agent. However, do not believe that a patent in itself will protect your business: it will give you a ticket to the law court to protect your position but do you have the money to be able to enforce it if a big corporation was to tread on your toes? What use are rights that are unenforceable? Innovation may be a safer defence.

If your unique resource is property, ie having the right property in the right place, which is often vital to the success of retailers, ensure that the lease is on appropriate terms, not just now but for the whole length of time you envisage in your business plan. A well-timed 'break clause', allowing you to take your business out of the property as and when you want without any penalty, may be as important as the right to stay in the property. Equally, a flexible lease in a serviced office rather than being tied into a long lease may be more appropriate to suit your changing needs.

In many cases, capital itself – cash – is the scarce resource that prevents others from competing. However, recessionary times have shown the dangers of financing an entrepreneurial business with borrowed money alone. Even if it is available, the repayment of debt can be an intolerable burden for an early-stage business. Borrowed money needs to be repaid – think carefully about whether your business would be able to service monthly repayments and hefty interest charges.

TOP TIPS

Generate cash as soon as you can by getting out there and making sales. Rather than perfecting your product or service at the prototype stage, sell what you have and use the proceeds to finance the business as it grows.

Cash is King. Too few businesses understand the difference between positive cash flow (when your customers pay before your suppliers are paid) and negative cash flow, (when your business' outgoings are more than its cash receipts). We will cover various aspects of financial management further in chapter 10.

ACTION POINT

Start thinking about how you can adopt a positive cash flow model for your business to increase its chances of survival and success.

4. Is the timing of the opportunity right?

Anyone who tried to start or build a technology business at the peak of the dotcom boom era in 2000 will recognise why timing is so important. Trying to launch that same business in the 1980s or 1990s or even after 2005 would have sparked quite a different response – typically met with either a 'too early' or 'too late' reaction. However, timing comes in three forms and it is rare for these to coincide.

Market timing

Ask yourself:

- Is the world ready for what my business is going to sell?
- Is the industry ready for this? The success of the VHS video format against the (arguably better) Betamax format because of market timing demonstrates this point very well.
- Will you be able to protect your position by being the first to move into that market?
- Alternatively, would you be better to wait for someone else to establish a market so that you can exploit it with a better solution? If you prove to be ahead of your time then you may find yourself undertaking the rather expensive and thankless task of educating your market, making it ready for your competitors to take control of while you burn through whatever limited cash reserves you may have.

Personal timing

Are you ready for the full-time commitment that this business will involve? Investors typically shy away from investing in a part-time management team who have other interests and whose time is diluted across various activities.

Starting a company is very straightforward, but once the company has creditors, employees, investors and bankers it is very much more difficult to escape. As the saying goes *'Any fool can start a love affair, but it takes a genius to end one successfully'* (George Bernard Shaw).

There are few more depressing sights than that of an entrepreneur who is trapped by his own business. The statistics for success in starting a business (especially in the UK) are miserably poor. The greatest cause of this lies in the fact that many ill-thought-out businesses have been launched with too little sense of timing.

Investor timing

Times of economic turmoil show us how quickly a flood of capital can turn to a drought. Since external finance may be required at various stages during the life of the business plan, you need to be confident that sources of capital will remain available to you when you are likely to need it in the future. However, good ideas almost always shine through and are able to secure finance…in the end!

ACTION POINT

Evaluate the timing of your opportunity to establish that now is the right moment to be launching your own business, in terms of the market, your personal position and the likely availability of finance as and when you may require it.

5. Does the opportunity constitute a scalable (and saleable) business?

Many business plans suffer from lack of ambition. This often seems to stem from the misconception that there is less risk in a smaller business which therefore requires only a relatively small amount of funding. Many entrepreneurs mistakenly believe that investors will be attracted to a modest business plan. Although a modest so-called 'lifestyle' plan may satisfy the needs of the management team to earn reasonable salaries, it will certainly not be appealing to external investors who want to make the 10 times multiple return on their investment.

Very often, this perceived lack of ambition comes from an incorrect view of the business' potential and a misunderstanding of what investors want from an early-stage business. Now that you have had the opportunity to evaluate what your business plan audience wants from your business, ask yourself if your business is capable of delivering these expectations or what needs to be changed to enable it to do so.

Entrepreneurs often spend too much time dealing with the day-to-day running of their small businesses instead of planning from a longer-term perspective. Consider not just how big your business can become but what the barrier to growth is –

if any! Research suggests that the greatest barrier to growth in entrepreneurial businesses is the shortcomings of their own management team. Entrepreneurs need to plan for a change in the management team and infrastructure in order to maximise the business' opportunity.

Scalability involves increasing sales without increasing costs in direct proportion – see the example below.

EXAMPLE

Company Z has developed a new software application which is ready to be introduced into the market for an annual licence fee of £100 per user. The company has spent £100,000 developing the application which is available as a chargeable download from 10 online sources. Company Z's overhead (cost) of selling 100 copies of the product is the same as selling 1 million copies. The business is said to be scalable as its overhead increases at a lower level than the increase in its sales.

Compare Company Z with Company W. Company W is a beauty salon that employs three beauty therapists who are each capable of undertaking 10 treatments a day and typically generate a maximum of £200 of revenue each day from this activity.

Company W pays each therapist £100 a day regardless of how many treatments they perform. Working at maximum capacity each therapist contributes a net revenue of £100 a day (£200 from treatments less the £100 daily cost of employing each of them). If all three therapists operate at maximum capacity then the business earns a net revenue of £300 a day. However, it still has a fixed overhead of £300 a day irrespective of how busy the three therapists are.

Company W's costs will put a drain on the business' cash flow if there is insufficient demand for treatments on a daily basis. In addition, if demand for treatments exceeds the capacity of the three therapists then Company W will need to employ another therapist at a further fixed overhead of £100 a day;

this may outweigh the value of the additional demand for treatments and will represent a disproportionate increase in the business' expenses.

In other words, the business will incur a higher overhead to keep up with increased demand. In this instance Company W may be considered as a business that is hard to scale up.

As you can see from the above example, it is generally easier for a product business to be scalable than for a service business. Service businesses, by definition, rely on a labour force for implementation and so incur associated costs and overhead in delivering that service. There are exceptions in some of the global consultancy businesses that have grown over the last 50 years and have specific processes in place to streamline their services along a production line, which uses their resources in the most efficient and cost effective manner. Generally, however, a service business will be well advised to turn its services into packaged products by selling the methodology that it offers at a premium rather than for a price instantly equivalent to chargeable man hours.

For example, going back to the beauty therapist scenario, Company W should explore the possibility of selling 'spa' days that include a variety of treatments, lunch and use of various other facilities. This can then be packaged at a premium price to leverage the full facilities on offer rather than selling individual treatments for which there is a direct associated cost.

Businesses can also make their model more scalable by outsourcing many of the tasks that in the past they might have done themselves. Examples of services that may be outsourced and so eliminate the need for a corresponding fixed overhead include printing, virtual telephone answering, and even consultancy resources which may be brought into the business as a variable freelance overhead. By doing this, a business can enjoy a reduction in its fixed overheads and only incur costs as and when the business is able to generate corresponding revenue.

ACTION POINT

Consider what elements of your business you could outsource without jeopardising the business itself.

Saleability

When considering scalability, you should also consider saleability. This is not to say that you should forever be wondering how to sell the business. By working out why anyone would buy the business you may also discover where the true value in the business lies. To start with you should consider if and how your business could survive without you, the entrepreneur, being in the business. If the value in the business is predicated on your skills, it may be very difficult to scale up the business as it will be difficult to find more people like you. Indeed, it will be even harder to sell the business if it relies on you, as who would want to buy a business where its main asset is no longer an integral part of it?

Scalability often involves keeping the business model simple. Many small businesses become too complicated with too many revenue streams, operational issues and management complexity. The successful businesses tend to be straightforward. On the other hand, you also need to be flexible in determining which path will be most scalable.

A less successful venture in e-learning (remote corporate learning by computer) was never able to determine how to scale its business despite having various immediately scalable options available to it. For several years, management discussed the business model choices – whether to build a technology platform (a scalable product), run a publishing business (again, scalable products), or provide a service to build bespoke e-learning platforms. This dilemma is common to many technology businesses and can only ever be resolved by researching the market generally, and the customers specifically, to understand if a scalable product can appeal to their needs. A scalable model is only an attractive option if it reflects client needs.

EXAMPLE

A great example of this flexibility has been shown by ByBox Ltd.

ByBox business model was based on a unique technology built into the manufacture of locker banks (traditionally used for left luggage). This ByBox technology allows them to change electronic locks on the locker banks from a central location. Initially, the management thought that this technology alone would enable them to build a scalable business rapidly. However, it became clear that corporate customers wanted a full service for both delivery of their packages and control of their stock and logistics by providing a remote access point for delivery of products that are kept on a site that is otherwise inaccessible by its clients.

By addressing demand and buying a delivery business to offer the two services together, ByBox has been able to build a highly scalable venture which looks likely to revolutionise the logistic systems of many large companies.

6. Does the opportunity offer good margin potential?

We are frequently approached by entrepreneurs who tell us with great excitement about their turnover for the past three years, and their prospects for growth based on this performance. When we start to dig deeper it becomes clear that their naivety distorts the difference between turnover (ie sales) and profit. Delving further we often ask our clients whether they are familiar with the difference between gross margins and net margins. Most typically they are not and, even more worryingly, they fail to appreciate why this should even matter.

Gross profit is the difference between sales (turnover or takings) and direct (variable) cost of sales such as raw materials and labour.

Gross margins represent the gross profit as a percentage of sales. This is clearly illustrated in the profit and loss forecast of XYZ Ltd in chapter 10 (p.129).

If you sell a product for £1 and the direct (variable) cost of manufacture is 10p, the gross margin is 90% (90p). However, 90p is not the net profit to the business. Fixed costs such as office costs, marketing, management etc, must be covered before the company is making a net profit.

The business' net profit identifies what is available for distribution to shareholders or reinvestment back into the business once the tax man has been paid. Therefore, it is crucial that you understand the break-even point of the business. This is when the value of sales after the variable production costs is exactly equal to the overheads of the business so that there is neither net profit nor net loss.

Understanding break-even

Break-even analysis depends on the following variables:

- The fixed production costs for a product.
- The variable production costs for a product.
- The product's unit price.
- The product's expected unit sales.

To work out your business' break-even point you will need to use the following formula:

[fixed costs] – [(unit selling price – variable cost) x units sold].

EXAMPLE

Company G is selling widgets. They have a fixed cost overhead of £10,000. The unit selling price of their product is £17 and the variable cost is £12. How many units will they need to sell to reach break-even point?

Using the formula we can work out that:

(£10,000 – (£17 – £12) x 2,000 = 0).

Therefore Company G needs to sell 2,000 units to reach break even.

ACTION POINT

Now apply this same formula to determine your business' break-even point.

As we will see when deciding on the best plan for a business, much is dependent on what fixed costs go into the business.

TOP TIPS

Use your business plan to work out how you can allocate scarce capital resources to fixed costs as efficiently as possible in the business.

Understanding gross margins will also give clues on how best to plan for the business. The software and pharmaceutical industries are examples of high gross margin industries. Gross margins are likely to exceed 90% as the product has been fully developed and so is able to be replicated time and time again with only minimal direct cost. In these cases, the key driver of the business is sales levels because for each £1 of goods sold, 90p of net profit is generated for the business. In such an industry, there is more scope to spend on marketing in order to generate maximum sales.

In the pharmaceutical industry, these margins may be protected by patents over the Intellectual Property. In the software industry, margins are likely to be protected only by innovation and constant new product lines.

In a low gross margin business such as food retailing or wholesaling, the key driver behind the business' success is to keep fixed costs to a minimum. This is one reason why the food retailing business in the UK has consolidated with a few large companies dominating the industry. They can then limit their fixed costs through a centralised facility (eg warehousing, marketing and management costs) and spread them over as high a level of sales as possible.

7. Are you developing an opportunity or simply an idea?

Thousands of great ideas are being generated on a regular basis. The majority of them remain nothing more than great ideas. In order for yours to become a commercial success make sure that each of the six previous 'tests' has been passed.

THE IMPORTANCE OF VALUE

In addition to passing these 'tests', it is essential that you understand the concept of value in a business. No business has ever succeeded without delivering value to the customer, and so at a very early stage you must establish what value your business is delivering, if any.

This value tends to come in one (or more) of three forms: saving customers' time, saving customers' money, and enhancing customers' lives. If you can deliver value on all three levels, the business will certainly thrive. If not then any one will suffice as long as you can:

- Deliver value.
- Explain clearly to customers what that value is.

ACTION POINT

The following exercise is one of the most difficult but useful exercises that a business owner or manager can attempt. You should try it not just within the business but with objective third parties.

In no more than 30 seconds try to articulate the following:

1. Who will buy from you?
Define your likely customer, eg ABC1 women (see p.79) across the UK with at least two children.

2. Why will they buy from you?
This is critical. Focus on customer benefits as opposed to product features. If in doubt, ask yourself 'So what?' and this will give you some clue as to whether you have articulated a benefit or a feature. The benefit is usually the conclusion from the feature.

For example:
Feature: The brand new washing machine from Bosch is able to complete a full wash cycle at just 15 degrees but without compromising on washing results or increasing the time of the washing cycle.

...So what?
Benefit: This represents a minimum 50% cost saving per wash by eliminating the need to heat the water to over 15 degrees.

3. How many will they buy?
If you have succeeded in answering the first two questions, you can start to consider the size of the potential market by establishing how many people are within your target market and providing primary evidence to suggest what percentage of them will be purchasers of your product. Researching your market will be covered in detail in chapter 5.

4. Why will they continue to buy over time?
Consider how the value you are delivering will ensure that the customer is tied into your business and will come back for repeat business. Consider the detrimental implications of a business model that is premised on a car tyre that never needs replacing.

Despite the huge size of the market, potentially quantifiable as four times the number of every vehicle that is on the road (five times if you include a spare wheel), the opportunity for repeat business is still much more valuable than one that is focused on a one-off customer. 'Annuity' income, which is paid on an annual basis such as membership or a technology maintenance contract, is more valuable than income which needs a fresh sales process each time. Think about how you can guarantee repeat custom and ongoing revenue from these same customers.

5. Why will they buy from you rather than someone else?
Start to consider why the value you are delivering differentiates your business from others which claim to offer the same value. If you are in doubt that others are offering the same as you, search for what you offer in an internet search engine, and you will see many others.

Try to come up with clear answers to each of these key questions.

In carrying out this exercise, bear in mind the following:
It is helpful for the customer to make a return on their expenditure, ie to make more money by buying your product/service than it costs them. For example the energy saving example above relating to the new washing machine would be very useful in establishing value.

TOP TIPS

Establish credibility by referring to case studies of success or the support of an industry guru for your business.

Sometimes you will have two levels of customer, both of which need to be satisfied of value, eg a food manufacturer needs to satisfy both the supermarket customer and the consumer; the magazine publisher needs to satisfy both the advertiser and the subscriber.

Understanding the nature of the value that your business is offering to customers will give you a very sound base from which to build the business plan and will play a huge role in how you communicate your marketing message to existing and prospective customers.

DARE TO BE DIFFERENT

There are many valuable studies of the importance of innovation in business. However, many business people misunderstand the meaning of the word. Before embarking on your business plan, you need to understand what innovation is and why it is increasingly important for your business to be different. As Jonas Ridderstrale and Kjell Nordstrom say in their book *Funky Business*:

'To succeed we must stop being so goddamn normal. If we behave like others, we will see the same things, come up with similar ideas, and develop identical products or services.'

Innovation is not necessarily about invention or new product design; it can be about novel delivery, novel distribution, novel service levels, a novel approach to a problem, or even a novel message. It is about making an impact. It is surprising how few businesses realise that they can innovate more in the delivery of their business proposition or their customer service than in their product itself. The best businesses thrive because they deliver what the customer wants, when they want it, in a manner that satisfies them. Consider how well your competitors are satisfying their customers. You can read more about this in the book *Simply Better: Winning and Keeping Customers by Delivering What Matters Most* by Patrick Barwise and Sean Meehan.

This is neither the time nor the place to analyse innovation in detail, but you will soon realise the dangers of extinction if your business does not move from being a price-based business to an innovation leader on a regular basis. The best businesses regularly cannibalise their own products and services before their competitors get a chance to do so for them, and the time delay before the next innovation is required is shrinking faster and faster. Make sure your business will be able to keep one step ahead of the game.

QUICK RECAP

- *Before writing your plan you need to assess your business idea rigorously.*
- *Does the opportunity match your experience, skills and interests?*
- *Can you recruit and lead the team needed to exploit the opportunity?*
- *What resources have you got that others are missing?*
- *Is the timing of the opportunity right?*
- *Does the opportunity constitute a scalable (and saleable) business?*
- *Does the opportunity offer good margin potential?*
- *Are you developing an opportunity or simply an idea?*
- *What value are you offering to your customers?*
- *What innovation are you planning in your business now and in the future?*
- *Only once you have done your groundwork are you ready to move on to start thinking about your business plan.*

CHAPTER 3

Timing, vision and background

This chapter looks at when a business plan should be written, how far into the future it should look and how often the plan should be updated. It goes on to explore how to start a business plan (with the vision) and then how to show the position the business is in now (the background).

The exercise of writing a business plan is certainly not a finite one and should reflect the fact that the document will change as quickly as the market around it. You will need to make sure that your business plan is kept current and relevant to reflect your business' needs, as well as your hopes and aspirations for your business at the various stages of its growth.

WHEN DO YOU WRITE THE PLAN?

In the all-too familiar 'boom and bust' life cycle of a business, it is normal to write a business plan at start-up, with a clean sheet of paper when the business has a whole future of excitement, aspirations and dreams ahead of it. It is equally essential, although less common, to write a business plan on the downward path, even though the management's time is scarcer as they juggle the day-to-day issues of keeping the business afloat.

Sadly we know that it is most unusual, but no less important, to write a plan when the business is enjoying success. When profits and cash are flowing, complacency often creeps in and there is a tendency to believe that this will always be the case. In fact only the best business managers anticipate that a product or service has a limited life cycle and that they need to keep planning for the next phase of the business.

WHAT ABOUT THE NUMBERS?

An important part of every business plan is the financial forecasts, ideally representing a mirror image of the narrative part of the document. The financial forecasts are used to show how the ideas and dreams of the business can be translated into cash. These financial forecasts should be revisited regularly, at least once or twice a year, and the assumptions that have been used to create the numbers should be evaluated to make sure that they are still appropriate and are consistent with the narrative of the plan.

If used appropriately, the numbers in the business plan will be one of the most useful management tools and so should be regarded as a critical feature of the document, regardless of the stage of the business' life at which the document is being created.

Of course, we all know for sure that the plan will not reflect what really happens in the future, but it is both an interesting and valuable process to look back at what has been planned and how the numbers have changed since they were created.

HOW FAR FORWARD SHOULD A BUSINESS PLAN BE LOOKING?

Again, in line with the individuality of each business, this will vary from one to another. It is common to plan over a three-year horizon; two years will probably paint an incomplete picture of the business' needs and projected performance, and one year is always too short to be useful. Equally four or five years is often too far ahead to be meaningful in a small business where changes in the market can create a huge impact foreseeable only with the help of a crystal ball.

WHERE DO YOU START?

THE VISION

Because most entrepreneurs are so close to their business, they tend to start writing their plan from the position in which they find themselves at the time of writing, ie 'this is where we are' rather than 'this is where we want to be'.

TOP TIPS

Start by thinking 'big picture' and keep focused to create a VISION for your business at the end of the time horizon you envisage, say in three years time. If you don't know where you are going, it is hard to work out how to get there.

The ability to capture in no more than one paragraph exactly what the business will look like three years from now is immensely powerful and valuable. Some people like to express their vision for the business in a mission statement, but this can be too 'fluffy' and full of business school jargon. However, a clear picture of where your business will be can help enormously to determine the best route to arrive at such a position.

A vision is made up of a number of tangible targets that you will know you have reached when you get there. A target is only of use if it can be attained, no matter how much hard work and dedication it may take to do so. A target can only be reached if there is a clearly identifiable end goal – one that can be measured in some way so that it becomes the 'end point' at which you can give yourself a pat on the back. An easy way to keep your targets focused is to make them **SMART**:

Specific
Measurable
Achievable
Realistic
Timed

The impact of applying the principles of SMART in practice becomes immediately apparent when we look at the following two statements which profess to convey the same message, but in very different ways:

'In the near future we want to have significantly increased revenues and have made more money than before.'

In this statement we have no way of determining the timeframe for this business to achieve its goals, or the extent of its forecast growth. When exactly is 'the near future'? Tomorrow, next month, next year? What would constitute 'significantly increased revenues'? Could this be 10%, 25% or even more?

The statement refers to an intention to 'make more money than ever before' although we are not given any idea about the sort of level of revenue that is envisaged, or the level that the business is currently generating so as to provide us with an idea about the existing and/or potential size of the business.

Now compare this with the following statement:

> *'In the next three years we will open 10 shops, increase turnover to £7.5m, employ 75 people in six sites across the UK and make a net profit of 10% on sales without increasing our debt. In short, by concentrating on delivering new products to customers and providing them with a world-class level of service, we will become the market leader in our chosen market of solar panels for residential homes in the UK over that period.'*

What a difference! Here we are given an exact picture of what the business is intending to do over the next three years, in terms of turnover, rate of growth, profitability levels and an overall vision for where the business wants to be in the market. Clearly this provides focus and direction for execution of the plan.

ACTION POINT

Prepare a SMART vision statement for your business to establish your goals. These goals will then need to be clearly identified within your business plan.

One of the best visions that we have heard (and seen being delivered) for a start-up business was 'We want to create the Marks & Spencer of childcare in the UK'. Although this may appear to be a loose concept, in one sentence a picture was created of a leading brand delivering high quality service consistently and widely across the country to a middle class customer base.

The best business plans are written after a great deal of thought about choices – what resources to allocate where in order to get the best rewards for the stakeholders, whilst balancing the extent and nature of the risks that will be involved.

Work out where you want to go and then decide how you are going to get there. Just like taking any journey, people do not leave one place without knowing where they are going to next.

Your business plan represents your roadmap – a 'sat nav' system for your business – which will determine your route to keep you on the right road at all times.

At every stage of your business' growth, each day, month and year, there will be decisions for you to make and choices that you will have to take that will invariably help shape your business' future. Without having the benefit of being able to test each of the options available, you will typically have to go with whatever you decide as being the most suitable option for your business at that time. Of course, you will never know what the outcome of the alternative options would have been, but by writing a business plan at the beginning of your business' life, articulating your vision, and keeping it updated on a regular basis you will have the opportunity to think through as many scenarios as you can. There is neither a definitive plan nor definitive answers for any business: there are many alternative plans available, and the challenge lies in choosing the best path at any one time as informed choices are typically the best ones.

Background

Once you have set out the vision for the business, it is essential to go back to the beginning and provide some background information to the plan. It is a common mistake to dive straight into the document without setting it in context, making the assumption that the audience not only knows the business as well as you do but can also automatically recognise the potential of the business. Do not assume anything. Instead start with a series of statements to provide a snapshot that will put the rest of the plan into context.

- When was the business founded?
- Has the business started trading? If so, how long ago?
- How did it originate?
- Where did the concept come from?
- How was the market opportunity identified? Did it come from your own experience?

- What has the trading history been so far?
- What has the financial history of the business been? Has it raised finance? If so, in what form and from whom?
- What differentiates this business from any other which has a similar concept?
- What is the current management team? Why have they been well suited to achieve what has been achieved so far?

The answers to these questions will create a compelling picture of what has been achieved to date and provide a platform for the future. As we saw earlier, you need to know where you are now and where you want to get to so that you can devote the rest of the plan to how to arrive at your desired destination.

ACTION POINT

Put the plan into context by explaining where you are coming from and where your business is now.

The following example is an extract from a client business plan looking for equity investment to support the growth of a natural skincare product range. The introductory information is set out in a series of clear statements to provide a succinct overview of the business' background.

EXAMPLE

(Extract from Infacare's business plan)
Infacare's current product range is aimed at babies and young children, and is a naturally derived skincare collection with no petroleum jelly, mineral oil, parabens or SLS, that is positioned within both the luxury gift and premium skincare markets to enjoy multiple market entry opportunities. The range is fragranced with 100% aromatic, organic, essential oils uniquely and especially blended to benefit the child. It is pure enough for both mother and baby. The range

was developed from Susan Kelly's passion for holistic and alternative treatments for herself and her family and from her knowledge of and belief in the damage arising from toxic chemicals in most mass market skincare products, especially as used on children.

Infacare Products Limited was incorporated on 1 November 2002, limited by shares, 99% owned by Susan Kelly, who has personally funded the business in its entirety to-date. Lucy Harris, who designed the Infacare logo and holds the remaining 1% of the company, no longer has any direct involvement.

The business generated a modest £80,000 turnover in its first year of trading, ending June 2007, and is registered for VAT.

Infacare is listed as a Trade Mark (Class 3) as of 14 February 2006 (Number 2,607,273), listing as Infacare stylised 'skin care products for babies and infants'.

ACTION POINT

Write a 100-word paragraph to describe where your company is now. Summarise any trading history and particular successes.

QUICK RECAP

- *The business plan should be regarded as a document that you revisit regularly.*
- *Do not treat the plan as a one-off necessary burden.*
- *Do not write the plan only at start-up and when you need it for the bank.*
- *Write the plan in good times when the future looks rosy so that you are in a strong position to tackle everything that comes your way, rather than be forced to negotiate and compromise when everything is stacked up against you.*
- *Create and agree on your long-term vision for the business as clearly as possible and then write your business plan to target this long-term vision.*
- *Understand that there may be several ways to progress from where you are now to attaining your vision. Consider the many different business models that can deliver your vision and then decide which is the most effective means of reaching your desired destination.*
- *Once you have articulated your vision, explain where the business is now. You will then need to show only how you are going to get from where you are now to where you want to go.*

CHAPTER 4

Describing your product or service

By the time they get to this point in the plan the reader should have a good feel for what stage your business has reached, but may have little idea about where you want to it to go. This chapter will show you how to write about your product or service in the context of the market opportunity that you have identified. This will help to provide the reader with details of what it is that you are selling. Later chapters will then explain how to write about who will buy from you, why they will buy from you as opposed to from anyone else, where you can find your customers and how you may be able to reach them.

AVOID TOO MUCH DETAIL

Avoid the common mistake of making this section of your business plan resemble something along the lines of a marketing brochure for your product or service. Of course, entrepreneurs are an excitable lot and find it easy to get so enthralled about what their business is that they are tempted to tell everyone about the features, the bells and whistles, of the business' products or services. However, the result is that the section becomes far too long, is littered with rambling technical detail which is of little interest, far from compelling and subsequently loses the reader at the first hurdle.

The key to this section of the plan is to start in the right place, ie build on the market opportunity that you have identified rather than trying to convince your reader that a market exists (somewhere!) for your newly invented product. For example, you may have an idea for a new cooking utensil that enables cheese to be prepared into wafer thin slices. This may be very exciting to you, the 'brains' behind this new gadget, but has the product been driven by a real need in the market? Is there any evidence that there will be demand for this 'next best thing' or will you need to convince people that their lives will never be the same again once they are the proud owner of this innovative cheese slicer?

TOP TIPS

Make sure that you can clearly identify the market before you design a product so that can you be sure that you are filling a need rather than trying to create demand.

DO YOUR HOMEWORK

If you are running an existing business and are looking to increase its product range, you will need to explain how you identified the market opportunity that has enabled the business to succeed so far and the market opportunities you envisage will sustain the business in the future.

Of course, the role of primary research (ie actually asking would-be customers for their opinion) to prove potential demand will give your business plan the reality check that an investor will be looking for at this stage. The process and importance of getting some first hand feedback to give weight and credibility to your business plan will be looked at in further depth in chapter 5, Identifying Your Market.

Before you launch any new products, whether as a start-up business or an existing one, you should ask yourself the following questions:

How can these market opportunities best be exploited by you rather than someone else?

In other words, what makes you better positioned to take advantage of a gap in the market which, if such a gap really exists, is likely to be quickly identified and jumped on by someone who is also on the look out for that 'next best thing'? Perhaps you have direct sector experience, which not only gives you the knowledge that you will need to turn your idea into a business, but may also have given you a very valuable contact directory which could get you that all-important head start? Perhaps you have immediate access to resources, such as funds, a manufacturing facility or a first class sales team to be able to carry this off before anyone else gets a look in? Whatever it may be, make sure that you can get – and stay – one step ahead of the game.

What value and specific benefits will a customer derive from your product?

Remember the low temperature washing machine scenario in chapter 2? So what? Ask the bill payer in any family size household what excites them about this feature and the economic value of this proposition shines through as the clear benefit.

How can those benefits be demonstrated and measured most effectively?

Do not assume people will take your word for whatever you will tell them about the 'value' of the benefits. Although most people can readily appreciate the implication of saving money, you may also want to consider alternative or additional features, such as the creation of jobs or social equality which are often described as 'outputs'. Typically these are best quantified in exact numbers such as 'the creation of four full time jobs and two part time jobs' and are often used as a way to measure the growth or performance of a business over a period of time. Another way of describing this is for it to be known as a 'benchmark' or Key Performance Indicator (KPI), interchangeable business terms that will enable you to keep your eyes focused on achieving more than just sales!

Why will the customer continue to buy on an ongoing basis?

Better still, if you have an existing business, ask your customers why they buy from you. You may well find some surprising responses, which will then need to be balanced against your own expectations, but will provide a very useful insight into why you have an ongoing client base. Of course, if you are just starting, you will need to make sure that you carve out a distinct place in the market for your business to separate you from anyone else. Positioning is very important, but do not underestimate the need for market-leading execution. We will look at this in more detail in chapters 5 and 6.

TOP TIPS

The strength of your client list is only as good as the quality of the last thing you sell to them – if you do not deliver what they expect in terms of quality then you can wave goodbye to that next sale.

THE DANGER OF COMPLACENCY

It is not unusual in a plan to see the sentence (often following a lengthy exposition of the technical wonders of the product) 'The benefits of our product to the customer are so self-evident that there is no need to explain them here.' Who are you trying to fool? Customer benefits are never self-evident and need to be clarified for the reader. Spoon feed the reader (who has hundreds of other plans to read) with reasons to invest in your business. This is rarely a mistake.

Let the reader understand the nature of the 'window of opportunity' that you intend to address. It needs to be wide enough for you to take advantage but not so wide that everyone else can follow. Again, we are back to making sure that you are able to identify why you have an advantage over everyone else which will keep you one step ahead at all times.

Whilst explaining the benefits – the so-called 'value proposition' – that you believe the business delivers, do not forget to put forward your evidence to support this. Is it just you that believes you have a solution to customers' problems (sometimes referred to as their 'pain'), or have you learned this by personal experience? Perhaps you have been listening to customers and prospective customers and, as a result, have crafted a way to help them meet their needs?

Finally, make sure that you keep telling the reader why your team is ideally qualified to exploit this opportunity? Many business plans leave a discussion of the key people until the 'People' section of the document. In fact investors will need a constant reminder throughout the business plan about the strength and capabilities of the people they are being asked to invest in. At each stage of the business plan you need to match the skills of your team to the business' ability to meet customers' needs. Is the design of your product revolutionary as a result of you having the best designer on board? Is the pricing of the product particularly competitive because of the financial modelling skills of a key individual? Do you anticipate introducing a refined version of your product every six months (thereby keeping abreast of competition) as a result of having access to first class engineers? Whatever and whoever it may be, regular references should be made throughout the plan to how the team is qualified to take advantage of the opportunities that are now available.

ACTION POINT

Using just two sentences make sure that you can describe what your business sells. Make sure your description includes the value proposition which underpins your product or service so that it is clear why people will want to buy from you.

THE RIGHT FLOW FOR YOUR THOUGHTS

The best products do not appear overnight or, if they do, they typically disappear just as fast as they were initially conceived. In contrast, a well thought out business plan should reflect a step by step thought process showing the systematic evolution of a product. Here is a useful model:

This is the market opportunity that I have identified

↓

This is my product to address that market opportunity

↓

These are the key benefits: the value proposition of my product

↓

This is the evidence that substantiates the value proposition

↓

And these are the people who will make it happen and why

Of course you do need to specify some aspects of the product or service, perhaps even a broad technical specification may be necessary; but remember to write it in plain layman's language that most people can understand and to provide any detail wholly in the context of the plan itself rather than being information for the sake of information.

So, if you are writing a plan to open a chain of food retail outlets, you should explain what the nature of the menus are, why the ambience of the outlets is different from others, and why the customers are going to find something more in your outlets than they can in existing ones.

If you are writing about a service that is to be potentially marketed to other businesses, eg an IT services operation, you will need to explain the ranges and packages of service and demonstrate that they meet the needs of particular customers. The fine detail about the IT systems that the business makes available and any other specifics would be irrelevant at this point of the plan. Such details should be addressed only if they represent unique features which create distinct benefits to the business' clients and provide clear differentiation for the IT services business. Anything more than this should be kept as an appendix.

HOW YOUR PRODUCT OR SERVICE WILL CHANGE

Looking further afield than the launch phase of your business, you should also remember that your product or service range should be changing over the period that the business plan envisages. You will need to be introducing new generations of products and product ranges. You should identify:

- When they will appear.
- Who will do the research and development, in-house or outsourced, again reflecting any core competences of your team.
- What the effect will be on existing ranges in order to demonstrate that you expect the business to grow.

EXAMPLE A

The implications of introducing new products within an existing business can be readily seen by this example of a fashion business which we will refer to here as Stage 21.

The business designs, makes and sells a range of bespoke women's clothing and is contemplating three options to fuel its future growth:

- *The introduction of a bespoke men's clothing range*
- *The introduction of a third party collection of ladies' fashion accessories to complement the existing bespoke ladies' clothing range*
- *The launch of a ready-to-wear diffusion range for women*

Whereas the introduction of a bespoke men's clothing range could open up a whole new market for Stage 21, the business' internal resource does not have any experience within the male clothing sector and so additional expertise would need to be brought in to the business at an appropriate cost. In addition, Stage 21 would need to identify how it could reach an appropriate male market, requiring money to be spent on advertising in different places to where the business is otherwise promoting its bespoke ladieswear. Does Stage 21 have access to money for this purpose and, more importantly, can it justify doing so seeing as the introduction of a menswear range is likely to have little, if any, beneficial impact on the core ladies range?

At the other end of the spectrum, the introduction of a third party collection of ladies' fashion accessories is likely to be truly detrimental to Stage 21's branded bespoke ladieswear range. The management recognises that the design and production of clothing are quite different from that of fashion accessories, since they require alternative manufacturing resources and have quite different cost implications. The inability of the business to bring on board its own branded accessories could potentially lead to confusion around and dilution of Stage 21's core values and thereby undermine everything that the business has built up to date.

In contrast, the launch of a ready-to-wear diffusion range for women who appreciate the value of Stage 21's bespoke range could represent a real opportunity for Stage 21 in the future. This could extend the business' typical client base, whilst retaining and enhancing the loyalty of its existing clients. In addition, and perhaps most significantly, a diffusion range could significantly enhance the elevated position of the bespoke range for those clients who are looking for something a little different. By engineering a difference between the two ranges, Stage 21 can justify charging higher prices for its bespoke range in line with the business' growth plan.

Working our way through each of the options is an interesting exercise which demonstrates that every business has a multitude of choices available to it at any point in time. Only by taking the time to evaluate the various paths available will you be able to avoid that wrong turn, whether at the launch or growth stage of your business. The beauty of your business plan is that it should evolve with your business and the opportunities available to it. You may choose to stand still, but everything else around you will continue to move.

EXAMPLE B

The following example has been extracted from a client business plan looking to support a bank loan application in order to launch an organic café outlet. The product description highlights the customer experience as a key differentiator relating to its product/service offering:

Consumers entering Café Fresh will walk into a fresh, bright, friendly place with an open atmosphere, offering a range of freshly prepared sandwiches, soups, salads and beverages, to be made available to either eat in or take away.

The décor will give a natural feel to the cafe, emphasising the very same qualities of the food. There will be a self-service fridge on one side and a counter with pleasant, welcoming staff behind it. The service area will be part of the counter and the salad bases and ingredients on display will be fresh and attractive. Café Fresh will be a transparent organisation that has nothing to hide, and so the whole service area will be open plan. Cleanliness will be a core part of the Café Fresh experience and the structural openness will be a great incentive to ensure high standards.

To buy their food, consumers will pick up a drink and sandwich from the customer side fridges and take them to the tills. If they do not want a sandwich, they can order the Café Fresh soups and salads.

Customers needing eating implements or the recycled paper napkins will pick them up as they move away from the serving area to take a seat or leave the café.

Everything will be on hand to maximise the customer experience both in terms of quality, speed, cleanliness, choice and value, reflecting all aspects of the Café Fresh brand.

QUICK RECAP

- *Describe your product or service in simple layman's language.*
- *Set it in the context of the market opportunity that you have identified.*
- *Do not make this section any longer than it needs to be – this is not a sales brochure.*
- *Concentrate on the benefits of the product or service to the customer, not on the features.*

CHAPTER 5

Identifying your market

Now that you have established what your business intends to sell, you need to explain who will be interested in buying what you have to offer. This chapter will explore how to identify and target your market. You need to provide information on your market context, market size, how your market will grow and where it is located. You will then need to show how the market you have described fits with how competitors make money, and how you can dominate a niche they have missed. This chapter will take you through how to present a clear picture of your intended market.

DEFINING YOUR MARKET

Having established how your business has evolved from the opportunity you have identified, your plan now needs to present a clear picture of your market in terms of:

Market context

Define your market correctly by segmenting the existing industry and explaining where in that industry you are going to compete and why. This segmentation can take into account environmental factors (grouping customers by common needs or location), regulatory factors (grouping customers by adherence to legal requirements), technological factors (grouping customers by how you might reach them), or demographic/social factors (grouping customers by their personal characteristics and/or buying patterns).

Market size

How many people might buy your product? Think in specific terms of exact numbers over a given period of time (do not forget to be SMART – see chapter 3). Do not make the mistake here of believing that 'anyone can be our customer'. You will have segmented the market by this point (see above). You should also identify your most appropriate customer and then work up from there to see how many customers have the same or similar characteristics within your chosen segment. This will be a better approach to finding your market size than reliance on general industry research.

Actual and projected growth rates in your target market

How big is your market and how may that change in the future? This will depend on some practical results from desktop and primary consumer market research. If you have a local sandwich shop, the planned opening of a huge office park just around the corner will bring at least 1,000 new office workers into the area.

How many of them would you expect to attract? Could you cope with this potential increase in business and what would happen to your business if another like-minded entrepreneur recognised the potential of this opportunity and decided to open up opposite you? Clearly the increased size of your target market would bring with it opportunities as well as threats.

Geographic breadth and variation

Where can your potential customers be found? If your business operates on a local level, whether out of a fixed retail outlet or on a mobile basis within a limited area, then you will need to focus on how you can target these local customers. Perhaps your business can be replicated across other areas, nationwide, or even globally? In each case your market will vary significantly.

In some more complex businesses, you may need to identify several separate segments of the market for several different products or services. Take the example of a recreational club which makes available sports facilities, beauty services, 'singles' evening Salsa classes and an after school teenage 'club'. Each of these services will be of appeal to a different target market – keep-fit enthusiasts, women, singles and teenagers – all of whom will need to be identified and converted into customers. Bear in mind that the channels to reach each of these targeted customers will also vary, as will be discussed in the next chapter.

Let us explore each of these elements in turn.

MARKET DEFINITION AND CONTEXT

It is a pity that so many business plans make the fundamental mistake of defining the wrong market. If you do not identify the market correctly at the outset, then the whole of the Market section of your business plan becomes vulnerable, which in turn renders the Marketing section meaningless (as that is built on assumptions about your target market – see chapter 6).

You need to define your market correctly by segmenting the targeted industry and explaining where in that industry you are going to compete and why.

TOP TIPS

A useful approach is to analyse your offering in comparison to current offerings in the industry by selecting the two key criteria, such as price and quality, by which customers decide where to buy (see chapter 7 on competition).

A good example of market analysis can be seen from the following extract of a business plan. This relates to the launch of a global software solution, which identifies people based on the way in which they walk (known as 'gait analysis'), almost like an individual's mobile footprint. The extract clearly identifies the nature of the total market(s) that this business, GAITPLAN, is to operate within, ie biometric security solutions and video surveillance software:

GAITPLAN EXAMPLE

'GAITPLAN currently operates within two large markets – the market for biometric security solutions and the market for video surveillance software.

The market for biometric security in 2006 was estimated to be around £848m worldwide, and is expected to reach £2.4bn in 2010. In terms of applications, Civil ID and PC /Network Access are and will remain the leading biometric applications over the next five years, expected to account for nearly £1.2bn ($2bn) in combined annual revenues in 2010.

Physical Access/Time and Attendance was estimated to be around £148m in annual revenues by 2009, with Surveillance and Screening applications estimated to account for £30m in annual revenue by 2009. GAITPLAN will primarily be used for surveillance and will respectively be positioned in the Surveillance and Screening segment of the market. The largest part of this market in terms of technology is the finger scan, accounting for 52% of the market, as shown in the picture below.

Worldwide biometric market share by technology, 2003

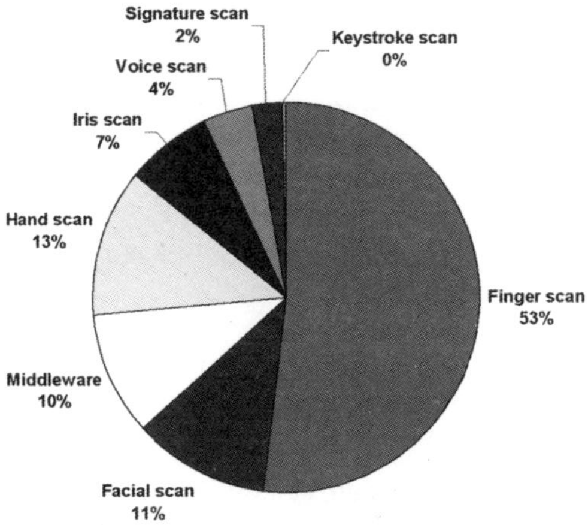

Gait is not reflected in this chart, since there are no existing practical technological solutions for gait surveillance and screening. GAITPLAN expects mostly to operate alongside the facial scan and voice scan technologies that are most suitable to be used for surveillance. Also, not surprisingly, the share of the surveillance segment of the market is relatively low, as there are no accurate biometric surveillance solutions on the market. GAITPLAN is expected to drive the growth of the surveillance and screening biometric segment of the market.

How the total market can be segmented into different markets

The global market for closed circuit television and video was worth over £960m in 2003[1]*. CCTV camera shipments totalled 16.18 million units in 2003. However, the global*

1 Karen Kin, Andre Chang. 'CCTV Industry – Monitoring Growth'. Citigroup Global Markets. September 2005.

market for intelligent video surveillance software (IVS) was valued at just £93m[2] *in 2004. IVS software analyses live or recorded video streams to detect suspicious activities, events or behaviour patterns. As well as improving the effectiveness of a security system, video content analysis also enables additional information to be gathered pertaining to loss prevention, public liability issues and consumer behaviour in retail environments.*

Despite its current small size, the market for IVS is projected to experience a robust double-digit annual growth rate to reach £406m[3] *by 2011. This growth will be derived to some extent*

from the expansion of network-based systems including local area networks (LAN), wide area networks (WAN) and the World Wide Web. At the same time, the replacement of analogue cameras by digital ones will boost the prospects of IVS software.

GAITPLAN will be operating as part of the IVS software market. GAITPLAN's biometric gait surveillance will improve the effectiveness of video surveillance and help reduce costs.

The identity and size of the initial market to be targeted

GAITPLAN's initial target market will be the market for homeland security, in particular the market of airport security.

According to the Federal Aviation Administration (FAA), there are more than 19,300 airports in the United States in 2001[4]*, of which 5,314 were open to the public. Among the latter 4,160 were publicly owned, while the rest were privately owned. It is expected that the primary opportunity for GAITPLAN will be in the publicly owned airports. Assuming an average price of software and initial system set-up of £150,000, this represents a £624m total market opportunity for GAITPLAN in the US. Assuming an average*

2 153.7 million USD.
3 670.7 million USD.
4 'The Economic Impact of US Airports'. Airport Council International. 2002.

support and maintenance fee of £50,000 per installed system, the potential annual market opportunity in support and maintenance fees for GAITPLAN in the US is estimated at £187m[5].

There were 3,130 airports in the European Union in 2004[6]. Among those 1,296[7] are with unpaved runways and most probably would not represent a significant potential market for GAITPLAN's software and services. Assuming a total opportunity for GAITPLAN in 1,834 airports, and an average price of software and initial system set-up of £100,000[8] the total opportunity for GAITPLAN systems is estimated at £129.6m in Europe. Assuming an average support and maintenance fee of £30,000 per installed system, this represents an £49.5m potential annual opportunity for GAITPLAN in the European Union[9].

Hence the total market opportunity for GAITPLAN systems in the US and the European Union is estimated at around £753.6m, while the annual opportunity from maintenance and support fees is estimated at around £236.5m. Beyond that there are significant opportunities for GAITPLAN's software in other world regions, in particular in countries such as Canada, Australia and Japan.

How that initial target market can be broken down further into sub-segments

GAITPLAN will initially target the market for intelligent video surveillance software in airport security for the busiest world airports. First of all it would target the 30 largest airports by international passenger traffic and the 30 largest airports by overall passenger traffic in the US and the EU. There are 37 airports in the US and the EU in both those categories[10] (see Appendix 1 and 2). Assuming that

5 Assuming that 10% of customers will not take on support and maintenance contracts.
6 http://www.indexmundi.com/european_union/airports.html
7 Ibid.
8 Due to the generally smaller size of EU airports than that of US airports.
9 Assuming that 10% of customers will not take on support and maintenance contracts.
10 Airports that are included in both categories are counted only once.

GAITPLAN would charge a software and system installation fee of at least £200,000 for each of these 37 largest airports, this represents a potential opportunity of £7.4m from systems installations. Respectively, assuming average maintenance fee of £75,000 for the largest airports, this represents an annual market opportunity of £2.8m for GAITPLAN.

The company will additionally target the largest international airports in the UK (see Appendix 3). Passenger traffic in UK airports has increased over 28% in the last five years. In 2004, the 62 UK airports have serviced around 216 million terminal passengers and 950 million transit passengers. They processed around 2.3 million flights, 2.4 million tons of freight and over 220 thousand tons of mail[11]*. With such an intense throughput, handling of security at UK airports requires significant resources. Airports' spending on security surveillance, terrorism prevention and crime prevention measures especially have increased in recent years. Despite those measures, there are often breaches of security, which are particularly worrying the authorities and management companies due to the heightened risk of terrorist attacks.*

The size of the initial sub-segmented market(s) to be targeted

Assuming that GAITPLAN software will be particularly useful in the UK international airports that handle at least a million scheduled passengers per annum, the company's target market in the UK is in 11 airports[12]*. Assuming a software and system installation fee of at least £100,000 for these airports, this represents a potential opportunity of over £1.1m from system installations. Respectively, assuming an average maintenance fee of £40,000 for each of these airports, this represents an annual market opportunity of £440,000 for GAITPLAN.'*

11 This excludes the three Channel Islands airports.
12 Excluding UK international airports that are among the largest 30 worldwide airports, e.g. Heathrow, Gatwick, Stansted, Manchester.

Luckily for GAITPLAN the company is in a unique position, having exclusive access to this technology and so able to dominate any market it chooses to enter. As your business is unlikely to benefit from this sort of market dominance, you will need to fight off other companies offering comparable products or services in order to gain market share. In this instance, you are likely to have more success if you find and define a niche where others do not compete. This is not necessarily as obvious as it may appear.

A market niche is often not considered to be big enough until a new entrant has demonstrated this to be the case. A good example of this is Green & Black's, which created a sizeable market for high quality organic chocolate in an industry where the dominant incumbent players, Cadbury's, Nestlé and Mars, had overlooked the demand for such an offering. History also tells us that IBM did not perceive the burgeoning market for desktop PCs until it was too late.

ACTION POINT

Work out what market your business is in. Do one or more markets exist for your business? Can each of these markets be segmented into smaller groups, either based on a narrower definition of the total market or the geographical implications of your business?

MARKET SIZE

It is absolutely true to say that someone wanting to open a chemist's shop in the High Street or a bowling alley in an out-of-town centre is entering the global pharmaceutical market or the global leisure market respectively. However, telling the reader that these markets are worth billions of pounds and are growing year-on-year is at best irrelevant and at worst misleading. More to the point, this demonstrates a clear lack of understanding about your business' prospects.

TOP TIPS

It is for you to decide how widely you will define the market that you are entering, although, as we have just seen above, this will be driven by the context of the market.

Consider whether Green & Black's is in any or all of the food market, the chocolate market, the taste market, the health market, the environmental market, the status market and the organic market.

Is it better to expand your market by selling more of the same to new customers or more products to the existing customers?

For any given market there are two ways of determining market size:

1) Third party, desk-top based market research

This is typically documented in industry reports from the likes of Keynote, Mintel and Verdict. (See Appendix 4 for a list of Resources.) Although third party research is usually expensive to buy, you can find a huge amount of information, often free of charge, at the world-class facilities of the Business and IP Centre at the British Library in London for example. Indeed, the British Library offers free workshops on the subject and even makes available a research facility to assist its users through the mountain of data on offer.

Report findings can be useful, but there are certain things to be wary of when using them. Specifically, you should make sure that the reports are still current and relevant. For example a report on the IT market which is anything more than 12 months old will be considered outdated in this fast moving industry. In addition, you will need to make sure that the report you are placing reliance on covers the specific market in which you are interested. For example, if you are opening a tea shop in the West End of London, information on global consumption of tea will not be helpful.

2) First hand consumer market research
   This will require you to ask a group of people (otherwise known as a 'sample') questions which will give you a real sense of the likely success of your business. This could be done by phone surveys, door-to-door surveys, or internet surveys. A sample of 100 people should be statistically significant per question for a market, so that a sample of 500 overall should give reliable results. The value of the feedback will depend on the nature of the questions that you ask. Consumer market research is vitally important regardless of whether yours is a product or a service business, a start-up or a mature business. Asking customers and potential customers the right questions will give a much better view of market size. These questions should be both qualitative and quantitative.

Qualitative research will create open questions 'What/when/why/how do you eat breakfast?' or 'If you came across this, what would you think?' This will help you to identify a real continuing customer need and to understand the reasons why people might buy from you.

According to Dominic Scott-Malden of Wardle McLean, a strategic research consultancy, quantitative research will provide an understanding of:

- Whether people like your product or service.
- If they would buy from you.
- How often they would buy.
- Whether they would be prepared to pay for your product and, if so, how much.
- What would be important to them to get them to buy again.

You will need to balance the cost against the benefit of doing the survey yourself and paying a professional firm to do so. It is crucial to ask the right questions. For example, if you ask Joe Public whether he wants a two-week holiday in the Caribbean you are likely to get an overwhelming 'Yes'; but if you ask the same question suggesting that it will cost £10,000, you will get a very different answer.

TOP TIPS

By listening to potential customers, you will be able to size your market from the bottom up rather than from the top down. In other words, potential customers will tell you what is important to them rather than you assuming that everyone in an entire market space will attach equal importance to what you intend to sell.

Once you know who your first or next customer will be, whether it will be a business or consumer, you can define their characteristics by reference to social status and demographics, geography (where they live), lifestyle, buying patterns etc. You will then be able to extrapolate how many other potential customers have the same characteristics.

Sweet Dreams' market

Sweet Dreams is a bed retailer which owns and operates a chain of six outlets across West London. The company intends to launch a top of the range Eco Mattress that is biodegradable and has just been awarded the 'Best Mattress of the Year' award for those with back problems. The mattress is to be sold at between £500 and £1,000 depending on the size of the bed.

To work out the size of Sweet Dreams' market, we need to go through the following process:

Question	Answer
Are we targeting businesses or consumers?	Consumers (on the assumption that the Eco Mattress will only be available through Sweet Dreams shops)
What is the typical social status of our potential customers?	Middle class – often referred to as the 'ABC1' population in terms of their profile and wealth. Sweet Dreams' target market will need to have access to disposable cash or the earning power to justify a three-figure 'discretionary' spend. In other words they appreciate the value of a high quality mattress instead of opting for a lower cost.
Demographics (ie how can the target market be measured in terms of characteristics such as age, gender, race, education and income level?)	**Age:** Four distinct groups (markets) who can be broken down as follows: 1. Young couples aged 25–35 who are setting up home for the first time and need to purchase their first bed and are driven by the 'eco' nature of Sweet Dreams' mattress. 2. Those aged 35–40 who have little time for themselves as they are busy bringing up children. 3. Mid-lifers aged 40–50 who wish to change their mattress and value the importance of a premium product. 4. Late-stagers, aged 50+, who recognise the importance of a premium product and are perhaps looking for a solution to back pain that they are already experiencing. **Gender:** Typically a mattress will be a joint purchase by a couple rather than being gender specific. **Education:** The 'informed' nature of the purchase suggests that the buyer will be educated at a higher education level, although this is incidental to the main purchasing considerations relating to comfort, price and (in some instances) the

	environmentally friendly nature of the product. **Race:** Typically immaterial as long as the customer profile matches all other characteristics. **Income levels:** the upper range price point suggests that the purchaser will be in the £50,000+ annual earnings bracket.
Geography (where do your potential customers live?)	The West London location of all of Sweet Dreams' outlets suggests that most customers will live in the immediate area. However, the business' market may widen out to other areas as the Eco Mattress becomes more popular, which will bring people in from other locations.
Lifestyle	Let's map the four age groups identified above to determine what sort of lifestyle each of them may have: 1. ABC1 young couples aged 25–35. These people are typically busy building a career and are willing to plough much of their disposable income into home purchases. 2. ABC1s aged 35–40 whose conscience and spend is mostly allocated to their young children. 3. ABC1 mid-lifers aged 40–50 who make calculated purchases based on the choice of alternatives available. They are secure as long-term home owners and look for quality with value for money whilst undertaking ongoing improvements to their home to maximise their standard of living. 4. ABC1 late-stagers, aged 50+, who regard health and comfort as two of the most important factors of their purchases.

Buying patterns	Couples aged 25–35 typically like to stretch their income to finance their social life as well as a whole range of various other household purchases. They typically adopt a 'buy now, pay later' attitude. Customers within this group would therefore look for attractive credit terms to finance their purchase to enable them to spend their income elsewhere.
	Couple aged 35–40 whose high financial commitments with schools, cars and holidays mean that they spend very little on the household purchases. Mid-lifers aged 40–50 are usually more impulsive in their buying habits, often driven by the strength of a brand. They are typically enjoying renewed purchasing power as a result of having a reduced mortgage, greater earnings and the increased independence of their growing children. Late-stagers aged 50+ are usually more prudent in the purchases, taking longer to make their mind up as they have more time to consider alternatives.

Clearly, therefore, Sweet Dreams should be targeting four distinct groups, all seemingly sharing the same social status and location but each of whose lifestyle and considerations are quite different. As such they will all need to be approached in a very different way if the company is to get customers from each of them.

To establish the size of Sweet Dreams' market based on the above we would need to work through the following steps:

How many households are there in the whole of West London?
For the purpose of this exercise let's say 2.5 million (although you would need to verify this using the most recent national census figures, available either online or through your local library).

How many of these can be classified as ABC1 households?
This provides the number of total 'qualifying' households within the appropriate area. Even if the census numbers show a figure of 1 million it would, of course, be foolish to assume that every household will buy one Eco Mattress.

By segmenting the 1 million into the four age groups, we can understand the size of each of these markets. Referring again to publicly available population statistics, you should be able to determine the size of each age group, refined on the basis of their being ABC1 in profile and living somewhere in West London.

For the sake of this exercise only (but not an assumption that you would make in reality!), let us suggest that the total 1 million market is made up of four equal quarters representing each of the age groups referred to above. This means that each target market comprises 250,000 households.

Market size and conversion rates

Now we can start to build a picture of how many of these we should be able to convert into customers based upon what we know about them and how they each make their purchases. For instance, the 'tight pockets' of the 35–40 year olds means that we can virtually eliminate them from expectations. This represents one quarter of the 1 million qualifying market which, as you can see, has already reduced the total West London market from 2.5 million to 750,000 households and that is still assuming a very unrealistic and unlikely conversion rate.

A further breakdown of the three remaining segments will provide more insight into likely sales figures although, in reality, nobody can be sure how many of each of the three groups will buy an Eco Mattress until the level of demand is gauged through first hand primary research. If we assume that a nominal 1% of the 250,000 young couples, mid-lifers and late-stagers will buy an Eco Mattress over the next 12 months, this would equate to 7,500 sales. At a price of £1,000 per mattress that would look pretty exciting, generating £7.5m turnover from one product alone. Realistically though, what grounds do we have for suggesting that 1% of our market will buy? It may be only a fraction of that which, of course, would have a tremendous effect on all aspects of the business.

Research and conversion rates

It is essential to undertake first hand research of a big enough sample group, at least, say, 1,000 people (ideally separated into each of the three target groups so that responses can be apportioned appropriately). This will give the assumed sales rate credibility in the business plan and have much more weight than the proverbial 'finger in the air' approach!

Of course, these findings are based on asking the right people the right questions. This is fundamental to useful market research and enables us to apply the findings to the market at large. It is essential to approach market research in a disciplined way. Make sure your sample is made up of genuinely representative potential customers, even though it may be tempting, especially in the early days, to ask for the advice of relatives, spouses and best friends. Friends' feedback is typically fraught with bias as their loyalty alone will make them immediate potential customers regardless of what you are selling, especially if they are not asked to pay!

It has been suggested that customers and prospective customers do not know what they want. This is generally a lazy way of avoiding the rigour of market research. Henry Ford is purported to have said 'If I had asked what my customers want, they would have told me "a faster horse".' This may be true, but asking for customer feedback is probably a risk worth taking. There are far more examples of businesses that have failed because they have written plans without enough first hand market research than ones which have not started because they have done the research.

Product companies such as Innocent (smoothies) and Gü (chocolate puddings) have demonstrated the power of handing out products for taste tests before launching them on the market. Service businesses need to spend time demonstrating their wares or giving them away without cost in order to establish whether they meet customer demands.

Spending some money on accurate market research in this way will be crucial to avoid the normal criticisms of business plans, that the forecasts of demand for new products or services are made up out of thin air. It is not difficult to window dress business plans with attractive sales figures. The inevitable 'hockey stick' curve (see chapter 1) will be heavily discounted by investors in the absence of there being any substance behind the numbers.

You will need to include the following data in order to substantiate the business plan:

- A sales forecast showing product breakdown based on real facts about consumer feedback.
- Any existing customer contracts.
- What promises have been made by customers and what their value is, preferably with reference to a past sales history.

EXAMPLE

Gee Shirts plans to sell 20,851 shirts in the first year of operations representing a total of more than £3m in sales. The unit sales forecast is shown in the table on p.85.

Number of Shirts	*Month 1*	*2*	*3*	*4*	*5*	*6*	*7*	*8*	*9*	*10*	*11*	*12*	**Total Year**
Jetsetter	250	459	1,112	1,300	1,350	2,000	450	650	750	850	950	1,150	**11,271**
Esprit de Sports	39	80	123	174	204	350	90	150	300	400	400	400	**2,710**
Khan	18	42	59	80	99	174	40	80	100	150	150	150	**1,142**
High Goal	2	4	6	5	5	10	8	10	10	10	10	10	**90**
Patron	1	2	4	2	1	4	4	4	4	4	4	4	**38**
Rehab	0	0	0	0	0	0	650	750	850	950	1,150	1,250	**5,600**
Total Shirts	310	587	1,304	1,561	1,659	2,538	1,242	1,644	2,014	2,364	2,664	2,964	**20,851**

Sales will be generated partly via online activity, but mainly through concessions in top stores, for which firm orders for the following four quarters have already been secured:

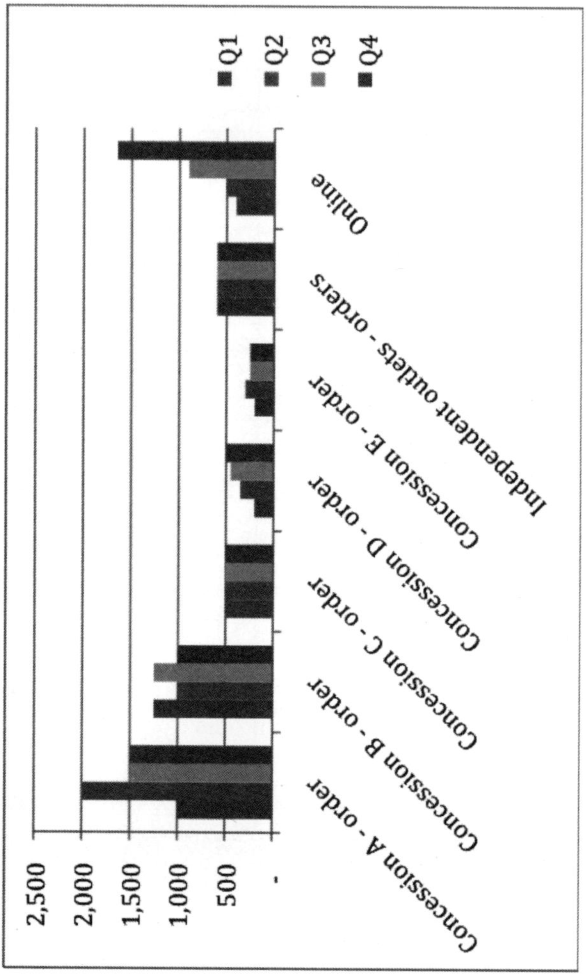

ACTION POINT

Apply the following five steps to sizing your market:

- Having identified what market segment or segments your business is in, work out who your first or next customer will be.
- Will they be a business or a consumer? What are their characteristics in terms of social status, lifestyle, buying patterns etc?
- How many other people within your segments can be classified in the same way?
- Based on asking a sample of these people, assess what percentage of them would be willing to do business with you.
- If you apply this percentage across your target segment(s), how many sales can you expect to generate within a given period?

ACTUAL AND PROJECTED GROWTH RATES IN YOUR TARGET MARKET

If you have an existing business, which has traded successfully and grown for many years, it may be reasonable to assume that the market will keep on growing at a similar rate in the future.

For a new business, or a new product or service, this will be more difficult. In this case, some speculation is required, some dependence on desktop market research, but a growth pattern can almost always be determined by reference to a similar product or service which has been launched in the past. There are very few products which are so new that they have no reference point in past products, even in the technology space.

Reference to customer buying patterns and past experience of product launches is very helpful in this regard. Above all, it is helpful to be able to quote a recognised industry expert, thereby providing a reality check on the sales forecasts and growth projections against current standard industry statistics. You will never get the growth rates exactly correct, but the key is to be able to defend the assumptions that you have made and demonstrate that they are rooted in reality.

GEOGRAPHIC BREADTH AND VARIATION

You need to assess how broad your market (as you have defined it) will be. This may change over the time horizon of the plan. We have touched on the importance of segmenting the market, and of avoiding the danger of assuming that 'anyone could be our customer'. It is equally important that your product should not be limited to the local market if it is capable of penetrating the global market. Either of these approaches could be equally inappropriate.

Approaching a global market from the start will absorb huge marketing resources; approaching too narrow a market will not exploit the window of opportunity which others may seize if you are too cautious. If you have confidence in your business then why not think big? A business that is capable of exciting growth should certainly feel justified in going beyond the local territory which it has comfortably operated in until now. Staying small may satisfy your ambitions, but it may make the business more vulnerable.

Treading a careful path between cautious and over-zealous 'traps' is essential in a business plan. Defending your decision to choose a particular path out of the many that are possible may make the difference between success and failure in the plan. Identifying key milestones at which your market can be widened may demonstrate the critical moments at which extra capital will be required.

But what about making money...?

Having worked out who you are going to be selling to and how many are likely to buy from you, you will now need to address the fundamental part of your business plan, which is to understand how you can make money from the market you have identified.

COMPETITION

You will need to go into depth about your competition later on in your business plan (see Chapter 7). For now, however, you will need to refer to it when you explain the basis for your strategy for entering your identified market. Because you will be making choices about where, when and how you compete, you need to show how your plans fit with the way other businesses make money in the market, and what they have missed that you will capitalise on.

Price

One major consideration will be how you are going to price your products and services. By adopting a strategy which places your business at the top end of the spectrum, you will be working in – and competing in – this premier end of the market. Many businesses underprice their offering because they mistakenly assume that this will enable them to enter the wider market successfully. However, price is rarely the main factor in buying decisions. If you have an innovative product or a higher quality service than what is currently on offer, customers will be inclined to pay a premium for it.

Providing a menu of products/services and prices is a valuable aspect of a business plan, but an explanation of how the prices and margins can be sustained over time is even more valuable.

What will your discounting strategy be? Is that part of your market entry strategy?

Quality

People typically value something more if it comes with a higher price tag, although quality (or innovation) will still be required to justify their additional spend. If you are offering an undifferentiated product similar to what is already available, customers are likely to stick to brands with which they are familiar.

Innovation

What will your response be to other people's attempts to follow your lead? As ever, at the core of your offering there needs to be innovation to meet or drive changing market needs: not just now but for the foreseeable future.

TOP TIPS

The best companies are thinking about their next generation of products whilst their current offering is still successful. Demonstrating that you have not just a product range now but a pipeline of new products throughout the life of the plan will mark your business model out as valid in the longer term.

Meeting customer expectations

While you are contemplating your business' place in the market, refer back to the value proposition that we looked at in chapter 2. This will provide you with the focus to ensure that you keep your customers' needs in mind rather than giving them a series of products that are exciting only to you. While many readers of this book may not remember the huge success of the first Amstrad stacked hi-fi systems, even fewer people will be familiar with the range of fancy electronic gadgets that Sir Alan Sugar mistakenly identified as being 'the next big thing'. The value proposition of all-in-one Amstrad music centres was a key factor behind the company's early success, but the company failed to replicate this with the Amstrad E-m@iler Plus Superphone and the Integra Face Care System. Whilst the Superphone was within the technology sector, and therefore within Amstrad customers' expectations, it failed to meet customer needs because it provided a service which was prohibitively expensive at a time when cost-effective alternatives were already available. The Face Care System, regardless of its youth enhancing properties, was completely out of context with Amstrad's focus on office technology. Both failed to replicate Amstrad's core value – whether in respect of customer needs and/or customer expectations.

Repeat business

Why will your customers continue to buy over time? The analogy of a software sale with a support contract may be useful. In any case, licence income or repeat business is very much more valuable than a business which brings in one-off purchases.

Finally, you will need to determine why your customers will buy from you rather than anyone else. Have you got a differentiated product or service? If so, is that just your opinion or do you have objective evidence from impartial third parties?

FORECASTING IN GOOD TIMES AND BAD TIMES

How do you make projections about your market to account for changes in the wider economy? The economy may lurch from boom to bust, which may in turn make people nervous and uncertain about the future. As we have seen, timing is critical to the success of a small business. However, the impact of the general economy on small companies is likely to be dwarfed over a three year period by the opportunities to take market share from others even in times of economic turmoil.

QUICK RECAP

- *Determine the size of the market starting with the first customer.*
- *Spend time and, if necessary, money on primary consumer market research.*
- *Do not work backwards from unsuitable desktop research.*
- *Take care in defining your market. Your business is likely to be in a relatively small niche of a much larger market.*
- *Segment the overall market starting with the group of customers which is most attractive to your business.*
- *Explain why you have identified the market as you have by describing how other providers make money in the market and what they have missed.*
- *Focus on dominating your chosen niche and the fluctuations of the wider economy through boom and bust will be less important.*

CHAPTER 6

Route to market: promotion, sales and distribution

Generally, the most difficult challenge for a company is finding a bridge by which they can link their offering to the market at an economic cost through promotion, sales and distribution. As we will see in this chapter, this is about making choices: you can reach your market in a number of different ways but each has a different risk profile and a different cost attached to it.

The three key areas in this section are:

- Promotion
- Sales
- Distribution

Promotion is about getting an interest; sales are about converting that interest into sales; distribution is about delivering to the customer.

PROMOTION

Although it would not be appropriate to reproduce a full marketing plan in a business plan, you should consider and weigh up all the ways of promoting the business both now and in the future. You can then explain the key elements of your marketing strategy, showing how it enables you to deliver your chosen strategy. One of the key questions will be whether you are going to build a brand or use someone else's name (supermarket, technology partner etc), a process known as own-branding for supermarkets or white labelling in the technology sphere. There are tremendous advantages in building your own brand: you can create value quite separate from the profitability of the business. It is now a common business model to build a brand without any manufacturing capability. However, the marketing costs of doing so may be prohibitive and very long term, involving heavy advertising expenditure. It may be better to promote the business from behind an established market presence, a High Street retailer or an industry-trusted conglomerate. The risk of this, of course, which must be balanced, is that you are dependent on the third party to promote your product in preference to others.

You should also consider how you are going to build knowledge of your business. The internet has enabled viral marketing – word of mouth – to thrive and businesses to grow without spending vast amounts on advertising, but it may be hard to lift your product above the noise generated by others. For every runaway internet success such as Facebook, eBay and Skype, there are a hundred 'also-rans' that have failed to reach their chosen audience. Even if you decide to promote your business yourself, the alternative methods of advertising and promotion would fill a separate book, ranging from leaflets to television, from partnering with well-known brands to Google adwords. However, this is not always an easy path. Search engine optimisation can help to promote your cause above other similar ones, but there are still vast numbers of companies languishing unrecognised which felt that just by having a presence on the internet they would be successful.

TOP TIPS

Consider whether you can draw attention to your business through articles in the local, national, international and industry press. Will it be worth paying a public relations (PR) company to promote your business? Generally PR is most effective when there is a fresh story to promote rather than run-of-the-mill activity.

Network marketing is an alternative means of promotion akin to viral marketing, as demonstrated by companies such as Herbalife and Ann Summers. Using amateur homeworkers rather than professional salespeople can engender trust for a new concept, but it may give the wrong image for the business. These are all things you need to consider when thinking about how you will promote your business. For more details on all the different types of marketing a business can use, see *Successful Marketing* by Pauline Rowson (Crimson Publishing, 2009).

ACTION POINT

List five ways in which you are going to make sure that your product/service gets exposed to your market. Differentiate between paid-for channels such as newspaper and banner ads and 'free' routes to your market such as PR and press releases.

SALES

When considering how you are going to sell, think about whether it is appropriate to have your own salesforce. Do you have the skills to manage your own salesforce? Could a professional company do a better job for you? A salesforce is, in reality, a fixed cost and a headache if economic times are tough. Specialist companies offer to make sales appointments, rewarded on results. Other specialist sales companies will sell with rewards coming on results. What suits you best will depend on the skills and resources that you have, both people and financial. It will also depend on whether your product is too specialist to be supported successfully by others. Perhaps you need a team of consultants who will have expert knowledge of your product and industry? If so, how are you going to charge for their services? Is their support an essential part of your service? Is this, in fact, the differentiator from others?

THE BENEFIT OF REPEAT BUSINESS

Ensuring that you have repeat business is a key element in a successful plan. You can sell more of the same to existing customers or something different to existing customers. Alternatively, you can sell the same thing to new customers. You should certainly consider the value of an annuity-style business, whereby customers pay a licence fee in advance and renew that licence each year unless they have a reason to stop.

TOP TIPS

The cost of acquiring new customers is usually high.

Whilst on this subject, try to think laterally about how you can maximise sales. Consider the business model of Gillette, which makes most of its profit out of the razor blades rather than the razors; the model of Hewlett-Packard and other inkjet printer manufacturers making more out of the ink refills than the printers; internet-based businesses that build their value out of the advertising rather than the underlying material online; in fact, all businesses that make their profit out of the ongoing contracts rather than the basic offering. You may be able to turn a weak and uncompetitive business into one that ties the consumer to you with regular repeat sales.

DISTRIBUTION

Above all, determine how the needs of the business will change over time. Your business plan needs to address the coming years, and as the business changes so the appropriate method of sales may change. For example, companies often think that they will be able to license their products to large established distributors. More often than not, distributors will be reluctant to support an unknown product, and you will need to establish a presence by direct sales before they will be prepared to push the product widely to the market. If you do decide to use distributors, check carefully who will have the power in the 'value chain' (the link from producer to consumer via distributor and retailer). If you are not careful, the profit will be in someone else's distribution system because they have more control over pricing than your business.

When you are thinking about different ways to distribute, think about licensing, but also think about local agents and wholesale distributors because very often they have access to the customers in a way that will be too expensive for you to manage by direct sales. Sage is a wonderful example of a software company that has built a loyal SME customer base for its accounting packages through local agents' knowledge of their customers. These local agents are likely to be selling other products already to your potential customers either through retail outlets or directly. Wholesalers are also likely to have access to your desired customers, but they will be organised on a national or international basis, and they may enable you to reduce your cost of making a sale. Indeed, many retailers will not buy products from 'one product' companies, fearing that they will need the management time to deal with too many companies as suppliers. If you come in this category, talk to the leading industry distributor.

ACTION POINT

Calculate the costs of running your own salesforce against the costs of outsourcing the function. Then write down the pros and cons of this. Do the same for building your own brand versus using other people's brands. Thirdly, do the same for alternative means of distribution.

FRANCHISING

Franchising may also be a possible route to expansion for service based businesses. It can enable a relatively small business to grow fast without the normal financing required for building your own infrastructure. If you are going down this track, you need to be sure that you, as the franchisor, have in place the products, methods, systems, paperwork and track record of profitability in your (the franchisor's existing) operation to demonstrate that there will be inherent value in the business for the franchisee.

It will be evident from this short list of alternative methods for reaching the market that this area of the business plan requires discussion, research, perhaps trial and error, and consideration of resources rather than a decision to go down the most obvious route to market without considering alternatives

HOW VIRTUAL CAN YOUR BUSINESS BE?

The concept of keeping your fixed costs to a minimum and outsourcing many peripheral activities to other companies has been a constant theme of this book. In your attempts to reach the market consider carefully what your business needs to do itself and what marketing activities can be done by others.

QUICK RECAP

- *Consider the many alternative routes to market which are open to your business, starting with the concept of a virtual business.*
- *Is it appropriate to build your own brand or can you hide behind an established one?*
- *Alternatives will need to be addressed in each of the three areas of promotion, sales and distribution.*
- *Balance the costs of building your own resources against using other people's resources.*
- *Balance the risk of using other people's resources against the strength of keeping a grip on the customer in the business.*

CHAPTER 7

Competition

In this chapter we will address not only who you are currently competing with but also how competition might change over time and how you might create a defensive strategy to protect your business' position.

Many business plans make the mistake of stating 'this business has no competition'. This betrays a drastic lack of understanding of the nature of competition. We will address competition in two dimensions: first, static competition, which itself comprises direct, indirect and substitute competition; and secondly, dynamic competition, ie competition that changes over time.

TYPES OF COMPETITION

Static competition

Direct competition (the obvious)

Most businesses look at the present environment for competition. If I am running a coffee shop, what are the other local coffee shops doing? If I am running a software business, are there any other software businesses doing the same as I am? In practice, such direct competition is just one of a range of competitors for your business. This is just a look at what you (and everyone else) can see. However, the range of competition is much wider.

Indirect competition

Indirect competition comes for the coffee shop from the fact that the customer can make coffee at home. It comes for the software supplier in that customers can achieve their objectives in different ways. Indeed, for many technology businesses with new products, their customers have been doing what they want to do for many years without technology. For the High Street retailer, competition may come in the form of online low-cost alternatives.

Substitute competition

Substitute competition can be more subtle but equally deadly. Take Eurotunnel, which certainly has a monopoly of tunnels under the Channel. However, it became very apparent in the early days that substitute competition from the ferry companies would take a heavy toll on the business. The ferry companies changed their business model drastically, first by slashing their prices and then by making money out of duty free sales, and Eurotunnel's business model was left in tatters because they could not achieve the financial forecasts that they projected with unsustainable pricing.

In essence, the key aspect of competition for any business is the competition not for that business' products or services but for the targeted customer's expenditure. The jewellery store is in competition with the luxury travel agent. The software business is in competition with the IT manager's other budgeted expenditure. Having understood where the real competition lies, your business plan can address how to position itself.

EXAMPLE

In chapter 5 we looked at how you can define which market you are in. This needs to refer to the other players in the market. You can redefine your market to take account of who else is competing. Swatch is one of the great case studies of a business that changed its model to defend itself against competition. At a time when the Swiss watch industry was being decimated by the emergence of digital technology, Swatch bravely switched tracks to become a provider of fashion accessories. This change took the company into a completely different territory with much less competition.

As we saw in chapter 5, one way to assess your options for competitive strategy is to analyse the current market players by reference to the two factors by which customers decide who to buy from, for example, price and quality. Competing on the basis of high price/low quality is unlikely to be successful. Equally unsuccessful will be trying to compete using a low price/high quality strategy unless you have a very innovative business model. There may, however, be a niche opportunity that the market leader has overlooked.

You can analyse your competitors' strength by determining their profitability and their size, but it is worth remembering that sometimes the easiest place to compete is right in the middle of a market dominated by a large player. Spotting a niche which is apparently of no interest to a large player can enable you to create a valuable company. This is often the case in fast moving markets where large companies have much slower decision-making processes than small companies.

EXAMPLE

The launch of a range of fresh soups by The New Covent Garden Food Company in the late 1980s was met with confusion when the founders, and the business' prospective funders, tried to identify the business' competitors to enable them to position the company within a given market. Fresh soups did not exist at that time, and tinned soups were not regarded to be an appropriate alternative. Instead, research indicated that other fresh, yet ready made, meals provided a more direct comparison. Using this analogy the potential market for The New Covent Garden Food Company's range of soups was equated to that for fresh chicken kievs.

Beware competing on price alone, however. It is a mistake to believe that reducing prices is a sensible market entry strategy. If you have a better product or service, it should be reasonable to charge a premium for it, provided that you can market it effectively. Cutting prices will merely create a commodity war, which your larger competitors are likely to win. 'We are the lowest cost producer' is likely to be a more effective slogan in a business plan than 'We are the lowest price provider'. In a price war the most efficient producer will win, if anyone does. In fact, the winner is likely to be the business that innovates best. Cannibalise your business before someone else does it for you! Always be thinking about the next generation of products and services rather than the current generation.

Dynamic competition

If you want to have a robust business plan, you now need to look beyond the static current field of competition and consider what will happen in the future. How will your prices and margins stand up over time? Bear in mind the section on the importance of gross margins in chapter 2. As we saw there, gross margins are almost always eroded by competition because new players will compete on price alone if they are lacking in innovation. However, few businesses take account of this in their financial models.

All too often, gross margins are forecast to remain constant over time. How will the incumbent players respond when you enter the market? Just by entering the market, you are changing the competitive landscape. They will certainly not stand still unless your product or service is unsuccessful, in which case it does not matter. In short, you need to find a way to retain customers.

DEFENDING YOUR POSITION

Barriers to entry

Building barriers to entry for competitors adds real value in a business plan. This may involve:

- **'First mover advantage' by becoming the recognised leader in the marketplace and stealing a march on your competitors.** Compare the first mover success of Amazon with the less successful online version of Waterstone's bookstore. There were attempts to deliver an online book business before Amazon, but theirs was the first well-resourced attempt. In this context beware being the very first with a new concept. The saying 'pioneers get scalped and colonists make money' is not entirely frivolous.
- **Reinforcing your brand by spending money on promotion.** Well-known and long-lasting brands from Coca Cola to McDonald's reinforce their brand with heavy promotional expenditure.
- **Regular innovation, introducing new product ranges while your competitors are copying your first generation of products.** See chapter 6 on route to market regarding the success of Hewlett-Packard and Gillette because of their constant innovation. 3M is another classic example of a business which is dedicated to, and thrives through, innovation. From its full range of office consumables, including adhesive backed 'post it notes', to petcare products, personal care items and its automotive range, 3M prides itself

on being 'a diversified technology company serving customers and communities with innovative products and services'.

- **Increased efficiency to compete effectively on price.** Compare McDonald's' pricing and profit margins with competing (apparently identical food retailing) independent businesses because of their very efficient operational processes.

If you can pursue all of these elements in one business, your plan will be much more attractive than if you address only the static current competition.

ACTION POINT

Take a look at the simplified competitor comparison chart below. Make a list of your current competitors and the characteristics of their products versus yours. What do they do differently from you? How do you appeal to the customers more effectively than they do in terms of pricing, brand and service level?

Go beyond this to think about who may be your competitors in the future. How can you protect your business' position against future competing forces?

Competitor comparison chart (SIMPLIFIED)

	ABC healthcare insurance	Signal healthcare insurance	Admirable health insurance
Flexible premiums	YES	NO	YES
Covers smokers	YES	YES	YES
Premiums increase with age	YES	NO	YES
All hospitals available	YES	NO	NO
Personal manager	YES	YES	NO
Online claims	YES	NO	NO
Brand strength	Low	High	High

QUICK RECAP

- *Don't just address the existing direct competition.*
- *Consider indirect competition. Think from the customer's point of view and not yours.*
- *Consider substitute competition. What alternative ways does the customer have to meet their needs?*
- *Consider future changes to the competitive landscape both because of your planned actions and because of other changes, eg in technology.*

CHAPTER 8

Operations

In this chapter we will look at how your business produces and delivers its products and/or services. Much as we saw in chapter 6 on route to market, how you operate your business reflects the choices open to you regarding what fixed costs you impose on the business. Working out the key points in the operation of your business will help show when you need funding and why. We will also look at customer service as a key part of effective operations.

RESOURCES ARE PRECIOUS

In contemplating your options for how to deliver the business' products and services, you need to focus on where it will be most effective to assign scarce capital resources. This is the case regardless of whether your business is manufacturing products or delivering services. You must consider whether it is more effective to run a virtual company in which others are carrying out the operational functions or to have a company burdened with necessary fixed costs because nobody else can carry this out as well as you can. Much may depend on what resources, including skilled management, are available.

TOP TIPS

You may find this section much easier if you consider how virtual your business could be and what areas of the business could be outsourced to other companies better placed to manufacture your goods or deliver your services without jeopardising your business' value.

Choices in manufacturing businesses

You should start with an explanation of what is involved in producing the product or delivering the service. Labour, materials, factory lines, design, assembly, office space etc can all be outsourced and delivered by other companies or managed in-house. Sometimes it will be most efficient to start with one model and change to a different model as the in-house facilities become fully utilised and spare capacity can be introduced in a flexible fashion from others. Think about what is involved in producing your product and the costs and expertise involved.

TOP TIPS

Consider all the issues raised by the technical requirements of large corporate customers. For example, the food industry now demands levels of technical support which may be excessive for a small supplier.

Choices in service businesses

Service businesses might need to consider things such as whether they want to have their own call centre or can outsource this. They might need to consider how many staff, such as consultants, are going to be freelance and how many are going to be permanent employees.

Making changes to how your business operates depends largely on timing. The cost of implementing operational change often involves a substantial change in the whole business, reducing profitability in the short term and creating a need for cash. Fundraising often needs to be timed to coincide with such step changes as volumes build up. A business plan which reflects a three to five year period must determine when these step changes are going to occur.

TOP TIPS

Whilst writing about operations, do not overburden the reader with technical details. Supplier agreements, machinery specifications, detailed costs of labour etc can go into appendices in order to keep the main body of the document succinct and focused on the key points, which will specify in what areas and when money needs to be spent.

Consider other case studies

In deliberating over what choices to make regarding operations, you should consider one or two case studies of successful (and unsuccessful) companies that have similar business models to yours.

There is an increasing trend for companies to build brands without spending money on internal manufacturing operations: Cobra beer, Innocent smoothies and Gü chocolate puddings all outsource most of the manufacturing of their product. Similarly technology companies are outsourcing their code writing to India and Eastern Europe. Several big Western consumer brands outsource not only their mass manufacturing but even their design activity to others with relatively low cost bases in China. If you decide to do this, you must then ensure that you have retained a sufficient core of the business so that you are not entirely dependent on other businesses over which you do not have complete control. Above all, there is generally a big advantage in keeping the business simple, focusing on what you are expert at and leaving all other aspects of the business to people whose cost base is lower than yours and whose expertise is higher.

ACTION POINT

Make a list of all the resources you need to make and deliver your product/service. Arrange the items in your list into two columns to separate those which will need to be increased in line with the anticipated growth of your business and those which will remain unaffected or will need to be increased only marginally as your business grows.

DELIVERING WHAT THE CUSTOMER WANTS

Whilst on the subject of operations, you must give thought to how the business will deliver what the customer really wants. There is an increasing trend, with the power of technology to deliver it, for businesses to provide 'mass customisation'. This involves customising what you offer to customers' requirements whilst retaining a common underlying product. Several car companies have tried to do this with varying levels of success. Whereas in previous generations mass manufacturing was the means to create the most efficient product, now it is far more important to provide the customer with what *they* want than with what *you* want to give them. A classic example of success in achieving this is Dell, a company which revolutionised the computer hardware industry by enabling customers to order an almost bespoke computer, having it assembled within a few days and delivering it to the customer. In fact, Dell's expertise in logistics may enable them to expand their business far beyond the computer industry.

EXAMPLE

The Star Online *reported in September 2008, 'Dell may need to outsource PC making. This will enable it to focus on sales and marketing'. Dell has had to consider different business models in order to remain competitive. It was also reported that Dell needs to work out its best operational plan: 'Dell finds it very hard to stay competitive in the PC industry if it retains its workforce during the "off seasons". It has two choices: it can either produce other related electronic products, or sell its manufacturing facilities and outsource its production... Outsourcing seems to be the preferred choice, as the* Wall Street Journal *had last week reported that Dell planned to sell its manufacturing facilities worldwide in a move to restrategise and enhance its competitive edge in the PC industry.'*

ONE BUSINESS PLAN OR MANY?

Many businesses are really trying to run two or more businesses without knowing it, for example the food retail outlet that manufactures its own products has all the challenges of a manufacturing business (which it could outsource) combined with all the challenges of retailing (when there are many alternative methods of distributing its products). If it compounds this by also selling products wholesale to retailers, the business may have become excessively complex.

CUSTOMER SERVICE – THE BIGGEST DIFFERENTIATOR

When you are writing about operations, there is one practical element which is often forgotten but which usually determines the success of the business: how is the business going to engage with the customer? Customer service is a much-overlooked differentiator. Training in this area is vital. Many pay lip service to it; few manage to achieve excellence. When you see it, you really notice it. We have already recognised that one of the keys to business success lies in delivering value to the customer, whether in a product or a service business, and so you need to demonstrate that you understand how your business is going to stand out in this regard.

The case study of British Airways, when the management was taken over by Lords King and Marshall, shows a business in which customer service had been a joke. When all employees had been sent on a rigorous customer service training course, customers flocked back to the airline. On the other hand, Ryanair has never been famous for its customer service, and yet it has built a very successful business on delivering what a large number of customers want at a price that they can afford. In the food service arena, especially in the UK, customer service is at best patchy. Few companies achieve or even aspire to the example set by Pret A Manger, where training is an essential part of the culture. Understanding your market and delivering what the customer wants means different things in different businesses.

In the retail arena, it may be significant that the John Lewis group has an unusual partnership structure, in which all staff share in the success of the business. It is probably not coincidence that they are performing better than so many of their rivals. Tesco has for many years stolen a march on its rivals through the information it derives about customer needs and trends from its Clubcard.

The execution of a business' operational model is almost always more important than the complex product and market theories that may lie behind it. Therefore, devoting some time to describing how you can ensure that staff perform as the business plan expects through leadership, management structure, detailed communication, training, systems, rewards and reporting is time well spent. Do not forget that the details of such issues need not appear in the main body of the business plan, but if they are central to your business' chances of success and value they will need to be addressed in more detail.

ACTION POINT

Describe your operations from the customer's viewpoint. In what ways are your customers affected by excellent or mediocre operations?

To bring all these points together, the extract below clearly identifies the important elements of the company's operations, such as:

- The manufacturing process (outsourced)
- The relationship with the manufacturer
- The installation process (retained by the company)
- Site identification (outsourced)
- Specific management has been allocated to control of outsourcing
- Customer service is critical and is therefore managed in-house
- Technology (described but the details are to be found only in an appendix)

EXAMPLE

(Extract from Operations section, ByBox Ltd's business plan by kind permission of ByBox Ltd's management.)

Operations

All functions are in place for a successful roll-out of the ByBox network

ByBox maintains a lean organisational structure with the management team active in business development, marketing and technology roles. Strategic partnerships are sought where external expertise is required in order to keep ByBox overheads as low as possible.

ByBox has the key operational functions to grow its business successfully; these are summarised below.

A proven and flexible manufacturing capability

This is provided by Logibag SA at its ISO 9002 registered factory in France. Logibag will supply ByBox with 10 locker-banks per month during 2002 with the option of increasing this capacity if necessary. These locker-banks will be invoiced at cost although supplied to ByBox at zero charge or interest until January 2003.

Conversion terms have already been agreed if ByBox is unable to start paying the invoices at this stage. The debt can either be restructured and paid over a period with a modest coupon, or converted into equity at the prevailing valuation.

An installation and maintenance capability

In April 2001, ByBox acquired Logibag UK from Logibag SA, its parent company. Logibag is a profitable company in charge of maintaining existing Logibag left luggage installations in the UK.

Logibag UK is responsible for the installation and maintenance of ByBox locker-banks in the UK.

Site acquisition and survey capability
In order to build its locker-bank network, ByBox requires a continuous supply of suitable sites. This is provided through a strategic partnership with Baker Rose. Baker Rose's property arm has surveyed, and is now building, a site option list around the M25 followed by national modelling of a 300-location network.

Business development capability
Dan Turner works closely with the logistics arm of Baker Rose on a combined business development effort. This ensures that a locker-bank is only installed on a location if there is a suitable level of demand by carriers.

Customer support capability
Currently ByBox operates its own customer service in order to learn as much as possible from customers' experiences of using ByBox. This function will be outsourced in time.

Software development and hosting capability
The technical architecture of the ByBox network is illustrated in Appendix 7. All locker-banks are managed by a central server. The central server will be local to the country in which the locker network is operating. All central servers report back to the central server in the UK. For example, the ByBox demonstration lockerbank in Canada is connected to a local server in Canada which is networked over the internet to the central server in the UK. In most cases this is how international subsidiaries will operate. The architecture is robust and scalable, hosted at the Aldebaran facility in High Wycombe.

QUICK RECAP

- *Consider all the different options that your business may have in its operations.*
- *Establish whether it needs to have any fixed infrastructure or whether it can operate virtually.*
- *Ask yourself whether it needs its own manufacturing capacity or property. If so, what changes will need to be made in the future as volumes increase, and when?*
- *Explain what methods you have developed to excel at executing the operations.*
- *Do not forget that great customer service can make the difference between success and failure.*

CHAPTER 9

Management

In this chapter we will look at why this is one of the most important sections of the plan, and one in which external investors will take a detailed interest.

Most businesses realise that they will not function without management. It is, therefore, a surprise to find that many business plans pay least attention to this section, and management summaries are relegated to a couple of CVs in an appendix. In fact, it is crucial that the key management positions – strategy, finance, sales and operations/technical – are addressed in turn.

MANAGEMENT, MANAGEMENT, MANAGEMENT

First of all, this is not the only section in which management should be mentioned. In every section of the plan, choices of how the business will operate – product, route to market, operations, finance etc – will depend on what expertise the company has to deliver it efficiently. Therefore, in describing these crucial areas of the business, you need to work out why you have chosen to retain the role in-house or outsource it according to who is available to deliver it both now and in the future.

Next, a clear description of the current management alongside an organisation chart (see p.121) should include each person's background, skills and track record along with their present and future responsibilities. In most small companies, there will be gaps: identifying these gaps and deciding how they will be plugged in the future is crucial. As discussed in chapter 2, why you will need to be able to recruit and lead a team. Even if you can cope with all aspects of management on your own now, it is unlikely this will last in a fast-growing business and you need to include information in your plans for such growth.

ACTION POINT

Draw up four columns, headed **a) People**, **b) Experience**, **c) Skills** and **d) Functions**. Make a list of all the people who are involved in your business in column a) and summarise their experience and skills in b) and c) so that you can clearly see who you have on board and what they each bring to the business.

Make a list of the areas of sector and functional expertise required for the business in column d) and see who is ideally placed to fill each of these roles. Are there any functions that cannot be undertaken by the people who are within the team and, if so, how do you propose to fill these gaps now and in the future?

Organisation chart

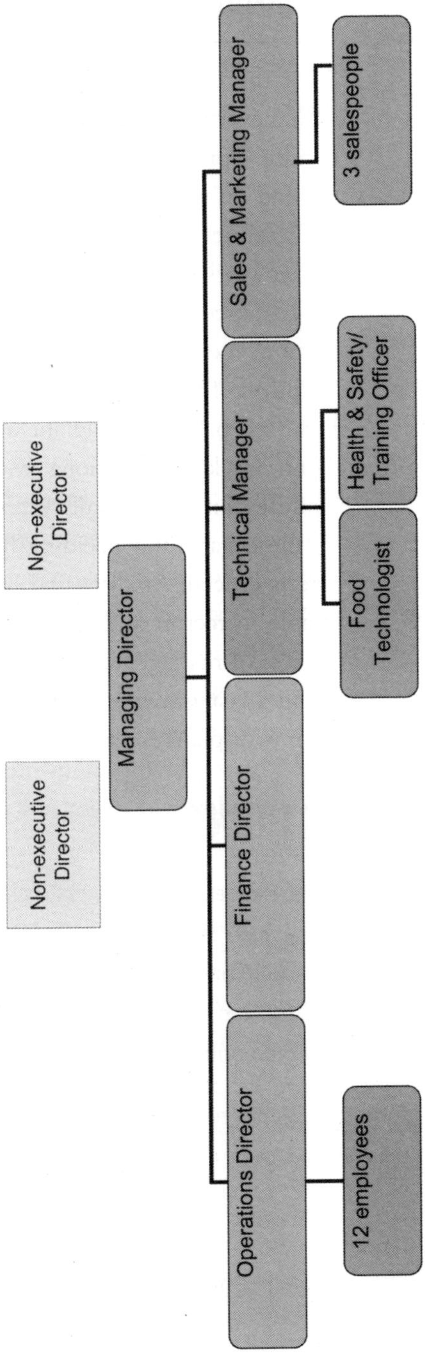

MANAGEMENT IN THE FUTURE

How will your management team need to change over time as the business makes changes in the next few years? Inevitably the present structure will not be appropriate as some managers are outgrown by the increasing needs of their roles. How will the role of the Chief Executive/Founder need to change? Introducing key people to the business at the right moment can make or break a business, and often external capital is needed to fund the right quality of person before they can be fully afforded by the business. This is something that external providers of capital understand, and it is generally less dangerous to take on external capital for this purpose than to let the business flounder because it is held back by lack of expertise. This may apply to the absence of a qualified Finance Director: a key role which can sometimes best be outsourced on a part-time basis. It may apply to a Sales Manager with international experience. It may apply to a Technical, Operational or R&D Manager.

Give some thought to when the founder of the company will step down as CEO. Most successful companies outgrow their founders, and businesses need to take effective action to deal with this.

TOP TIPS

Bear in mind this quotation from David Ogilvy of the advertising agency Ogilvy & Mather:
'If each of us hires people who are smaller than we are, we shall become a company of dwarfs. But if each of us hires people who are bigger than we are, we shall become a company of giants.'

EXAMPLE

The London Consultancy Group Ltd (LCG) decided in 2006 to adopt a growth strategy which involves management identifying and targeting owners of smaller consultancy businesses operating in a comparable area who would benefit from working as part of a larger organisation. The consolidation of these potential competitors in this way is known as a 'roll up'. The object of this was to enable LCG to be regarded as a much larger organisation since it would include the activity of all the other businesses coming into the group.

As part of LCG's plans to roll up smaller players and achieve its overall growth milestones, Managing Directors of the acquisition targets were invited to become equity shareholders of the consolidated entity. This way the Managing Directors of target firms could increase their regular income stream while gaining a viable exit strategy for their businesses. As many Managing Directors of identified targets were seen as being close to retirement, the management team formulated a five year succession plan. The plan was designed to exit retiring partners from the business operationally, while ensuring that their knowledge, contacts and expertise were passed on to junior partners who would be groomed to take on management of the subsidiary.

THE ROLE OF A BOARD OF DIRECTORS

Do not forget the importance of the Board of Directors. An effective Board can contribute massively to the efficient functioning of the company and a dysfunctional Board can have an equally detrimental affect. Small companies often forget what the Board needs to do. Patrick Dunne of 3i has put this as succinctly as possible in his book *Directors' Dilemmas*:

- Ensure the right strategy is in place and that it is being followed.

- Ensure there are the right resources in place to fit with the agreed strategy. The most important of these are human and financial resources.
- Keep out of jail... The board needs to ensure that the company complies with all the appropriate regulations relating to its industry and the countries within which it operates.

With this in mind, it is unlikely that the Board is going to function most effectively while it comprises only the most senior executive line managers. Building a sensibly balanced Board of executives and independent experienced non-executives (ie not just representing investors) can add real value to a business, especially where the Chief Executive is a dominant, if not domineering, force. The business plan needs to identify who the non-executive directors are now or who they will be in the future.

Another aspect for a business owner and management to consider and address, if the business is going to raise money from external investors for the first time, is how a founder/CEO's role is going to change once he/she is answerable to a third party. This is often a psychological problem when previously the founder has had total control.

TOP TIPS

At this stage reconsider the seven essential questions outlined in chapter 2. If you are thinking about selling your business in the future, how will the business be managed without you? What steps have you taken to ensure that there is a management team to succeed you? Even if this is not spelled out specifically in the business plan, any prospective buyer will want to understand how the business can be managed without you.

Finally, make choices about which 'employees' will be full-time, which will be part-time, which will be freelance and which roles will be outsourced, and give an explanation of why the choices have been made in each case. There needs to be a balance between flexibility and control.

In all cases, make it clear how the reward structure will incentivise everyone in the company without jeopardising its cash position, taking into account the alternative reward schemes of pay, perks, bonuses and options.

SHOW YOUR PASSION

In describing the management team, bear in mind that an entrepreneur's ability to demonstrate passion for the business is likely to enhance a bland description of the management team enormously. The characteristic of passion is often present in entrepreneurs but, particularly in the UK, businesses can become bogged down and lose the drive and creativity that we associate with our US contemporaries. In the US, provided that entrepreneurs can show passion, even failure is often regarded as an important part of their education that will fuel future success, recognising the fact that entrepreneurs are rarely bred overnight.

Disappointingly passion rarely features in business plans, which tend to deteriorate into dry, wordy documents. All too often we see business plans stripped of excitement and enthusiasm to become bland statements of fact rather than visionary and justified expressions of intention. Great managers frequently leave large-scale multinational corporations to work for early-stage entrepreneurial businesses, almost always because of the buzz, the excitement and the potential long-term rewards that can be available. This passion needs to jump off the page of a business plan to convince investors that the management team of a business is at least as excited about the business as they are. The example below shows one business plan that successfully showed both passion and expertise.

EXAMPLE

John Smith has dedicated all of his efforts to the ABC business for the past four years. He has personally committed all available private funds of £50,000 to establish the feasibility and further the development of the ABC concept. John has direct sector expertise, working within the barbering industry for the past 12 years, and running his own business since 2004, which has given him managerial experience as he runs the business on a day-to-day basis and employs a team of six.

John's primary role is to promote, manage and fulfil his vision of revolutionising barbering and the teaching of barbering in the 21st century. Together with specialists and the following hands-on management team, he aims to leverage his sector knowledge from both an industry and operational perspective to build a business making £2m pa net profit and to establish an ABC brand culture that is focused on personal achievement both inside and outside the organisation.

ACTION POINT

Write down five things which excite you most about your business. Try to differentiate between emotive elements that are specific only to you, such as the business being an extension of your hobby, and aspects of the business itself which are exciting, such as the opportunity to introduce a new product or service into a given market or to introduce an innovative way of working into an established market.

QUICK RECAP

- *The management section is the most important part of the business plan. Give it the focus that it needs.*
- *Consider not only the current management team but also future requirements and how the relevant people are going to be recruited.*
- *Ensure that the management skills are demonstrated in other appropriate places throughout the plan.*
- *Make reference not just to the senior managers but also to key staff and the Board, including non-executive directors.*
- *Establish the future role of the CEO/Founder and when it would be right for him/her to take a back seat in favour of a professional manager.*

CHAPTER 10

Financial assumptions and information

In this chapter, we will look at not only the technical construction of a financial model (including profit & loss, cash flow and balance sheet forecasts) but also how the financial section needs to be related to the words of the plan. This connection, explaining the assumptions that link the words to the numbers, will clarify the business model.

We will also look at alternative forms of finance and how they need to be repaid.

LEARNING THE FINANCIAL ROPES

Accountants can sometimes give the impression that accounts, financial models and forecasts are aspects of a dark art which is hard for a busy entrepreneur to understand. In fact, the key elements of a financial model are relatively simple, and it is absolutely vital in a small business that all the senior management understand them. If you are daunted by your lack of knowledge on financial modelling and accounts, there are a number of courses available along the lines of 'Finance for non-financial managers'. This is a good use of a day or two of your time.

If you are put off by the technical aspects of constructing a financial model for the business plan, subcontract it to someone else. However, do not subcontract the necessary work that will be done on the assumptions that lie behind it, for example the sales forecast. We will focus here on the elements that you must address and understand as the business manager.

SPREADSHEETS

The ease with which software such as MS-Excel can manipulate financial models makes it tempting to provide reams of numbers. However, this is not helpful in a business plan and is likely to be highly distracting.

A good plan will include the following elements:

- Profit & loss forecast, cash flow forecast and balance sheet forecast for the next three years, broken down into monthly forecasts for the first year and quarterly forecasts for the second and third years.
- One or, at most, two sensitivity analyses, showing the same basic business and the same basic spreadsheet but demonstrating what would happen in the instance of a change in certain expectations. This will be useful only if it shows the key changes in any given business, for example

what will happen to the figures with a 10% drop in sales or a 2% drop in gross margins in a business with high gross margins, or a 10% increase in fixed costs in a business with low gross margins.
- An explanation of the break-even level for the business at various stages of its development.

Any more information than this is likely to confuse rather than support the business plan.

From this information it should be possible to extract how much money the business will require in the future, but remember to allow a cushion for the inevitable mishaps that will occur. It is a common mistake to ask for exactly the amount of money that the cash flow forecast demonstrates; investors understand that a cash reserve will almost certainly be needed.

For an existing business that has a trading history, start with some simplified audited and/or management accounts showing the track record of trading in recent months or years.

TOP TIPS

Keep the number of spreadsheets to a minimum. Excessive information distracts the reader from the core message.

ESSENTIAL ELEMENTS

For all businesses, the following elements will be essential.

Cash flow

The cash flow forecast will demonstrate how much money you will need and when.

The lifeblood of any business, but especially a small early-stage one, is cash. Therefore, understanding the difference between a profit & loss forecast and a cash flow forecast is very important.

The **profit & loss forecast** is an accounting device to determine profit over a period; the **cash flow forecast** shows how the cash comes into and goes out of the business. This difference can be summed up in one word – *timing* – and it may determine survival for your business. If your company cannot pay its debts and obligations when they become due, it will become insolvent and unable to trade. Hence, it is vital that a business plan (however good its theory) includes a defensible cash flow forecast.

The impact cash flow can have on your business can be illustrated by looking at the different ways you can sell your product or service:

1) You sell your product or service and at the same time you invoice for it and get paid. In such an example, the profit & loss account and the cash flow reporting will be the same.
2) You sell your product or service on credit (say 30 day terms). You deliver and invoice on day 1 and on day 30 (or more often day 45 or even 60 if the terms are 30 days from the end of the month following the invoice) you get paid. This is negative cash flow and needs to be monitored very carefully. It can lead to 'overtrading', which is the cause of more businesses going bankrupt than lack of sales: essentially the business is successful and grows too fast for the cash reserves that it has. Suppliers and employees need to be paid before cash is received from customers and the bank will not support the shortfall. Negative cash flow can also cause problems with bad debts. Invoicing customers can give the impression of a successful business, but the transaction cycle is not complete until the invoice has been paid.
3) You sell your product or service but get paid in advance of delivering the product by, say, 30 days. This is positive cash flow and, in many businesses is the main way to finance the operations. Consider the insurance business model, where

much of the money is made from investing premiums. Consider also the bespoke furniture business, where a deposit is taken in advance, or the retail business, the greatest attraction of which is the fact that cash comes into the till from the customers, and suppliers can be paid on credit.

The other side of this cash flow picture is the timing of supplier payments. If you can possibly persuade suppliers to extend credit to you and allow you to pay a long time after the goods are delivered, you may not need to raise external finance because your suppliers will be financing your business.

The timing of supplier and customer payments will affect 'working capital'. This measures how much in 'liquid assets', ie cash and other assets, such as payments due from customers which can easily be turned into cash, a company has available to build its business. The number can be positive or negative, depending on how much debt the company has. In general, companies that have a lot of working capital will be more successful since they can expand and improve their operations more easily.

In addition to these working capital requirements, you will need to show that you have included in the cash flow forecast any capital repayments on finance leases or bank debt. VAT (Value Added Tax) and PAYE (Pay As You Earn, the HMRC's system for collecting income tax and National Insurance at the source of payment – ie before the employee receives it) timing should also be included if they are paid at a significantly different time from the original purchase and payroll respectively. Finally, ensure that you include a repayment schedule for any debt you intend to take on in the future.

So, whereas the profit & loss forecast will obscure the flow of cash because of accruals and prepayments (supplier invoices paid in advance or arrears), the cash flow forecast will be a true reflection of how much money the business needs to survive.

TOP TIPS

Do not overcomplicate the cash flow forecast with multiple unnecessary rows. Bear in mind what the reader needs to know in order to understand where the cash comes from and goes. This will include:

- Sales receipts (bearing in mind seasonal factors)
- Supplier payments (reflecting stock movement)
- Payroll
- Tax payments
- Overhead payments at the time they are made
- Interest and capital payments to lenders, eg the bank

From this cash flow forecast you will be able to assess who would be the most suitable provider of finance and in what form, for example an overdraft or loan from a bank, or new equity from shareholders. An overdraft would be more suitable if a deficit of cash is only temporary due to seasonal factors. See the section on raising finance on p.142.

It is a good idea to leave yourself sufficient cash to provide a margin for error, making the reasonable assumption that not all of your forecasts will be accurate. Err on the cautious side and leave your business with a safety cushion of cash. Raising finance is likely to take longer than you think and you may need that buffer. In the case of XYZ Ltd, a start-up manufacturing business, shown on p.135, an overdraft facility of at least £100,000 would be recommended to cover the expected maximum cash deficit of £70,694 shown in December 2008.

XYZ Limited											
Projected cashflow											
	Jul-08	Aug-08	Sep-08	Oct-08	Nov-08	Dec-08	Q1 2009	Q2 2009	TOTAL 2008-9	2009-10	2010-11
INCOMING FUNDS											
Issue of shares	625,000	625,000							1,250,000		
Bank loan			400,000	250,000					650,000		
Sales receipts				0	180,000	360,000	1,440,000	1,560,000	3,540,000	6,810,000	7,575,000
VAT reclaimable			2,695	90,353	92,024	72,678	58,354	72,914	389,016	339,771	372,759
TOTAL	**625,000**	**625,000**	**402,695**	**340,353**	**272,024**	**432,678**	**1,498,354**	**1,632,914**	**5,829,016**	**7,149,771**	**7,947,759**
OUTGOING FUNDS											
Capital expenditure		500,000	500,000	350,000					1,350,000	150,000	150,000
Supplier payments				122,500	140,000	182,000	726,000	786,000	1,956,500	3,429,000	3,811,500
Payroll		16,650	51,300	95,940	122,940	146,925	428,805	428,805	1,291,365	1,929,660	2,144,020
Overheads	15,400	16,300	25,850	31,000	46,600	69,050	194,650	198,250	597,100	868,700	950,050
Input VAT	2,695	90,353	92,024	72,678	15,015	20,904	69,344	72,914	435,925	345,118	378,096
Bank costs			8,000	3,600	8,000	8,720	22,222	21,581	72,123	65,210	40,098
Corporation tax											55,837
Bank repayments					7,000	7,000	21,000	21,000	56,000	184,800	184,800
TOTAL	**18,095**	**623,303**	**677,174**	**675,718**	**339,555**	**434,599**	**1,462,021**	**1,528,550**	**5,759,013**	**6,972,488**	**7,714,401**
NET CASH SURPLUS/(DEFICIT)	**606,905**	**1,697**	**-274,479**	**-335,365**	**-67,531**	**-1,921**	**36,333**	**104,364**	**70,003**	**177,283**	**233,358**
CUM CASH SURPLUS/(DEFICIT)	**606,905**	**608,602**	**334,123**	**-1,242**	**-68,773**	**-70,694**	**-34,361**	**70,003**		**247,286**	**480,644**

ACTION POINT

Prepare a month-by-month cash flow forecast to show when and how cash is generated and spent. Make sure that you understand the difference between the business' cash position and gross/net profitability. If in doubt, ask a financial adviser or accountant.

Profit & loss

Sales, revenue and turnover (all terms which are used to mean the same thing) drive cash into a business, and so the sales forecast is probably the most important aspect of a financial model. But beware, in most cases it is the least thought out or defensible aspect.

The sales forecast will be the top line of your profit & loss forecast (see the example on p.138) In a well-established business, which has a track record of sales, it may be reasonable to project future sales from past history, but in a relatively new business or one that is creating new products or services such projections will not be possible.

If you can provide a sales pipeline showing contracts won, orders promised, customers contacted etc, do so. They give much-needed credibility to the sales forecast. If, as is likely, this pipeline is shaky, you must fall back on expectations based on market research. This comprises both desktop research of market potential and growth and, more importantly, first hand customer research. Documenting this research in a way that is convincing will add hugely to the persuasiveness of the forecast (see chapter 5).

Projecting sales forecasts out of thin air will destroy any value generated by the hard work put into the rest of the plan. Once a realistic sales forecast has been created, you can focus on the gross margins that the business will sustain, breaking these down by product or service lines if it is appropriate to do so.

TOP TIPS

Remember from chapter 2 that gross profit represents the difference between sales and direct cost of sales in materials and labour, and gross margins show this figure as a percentage of sales. See the example profit & loss forecast for XYZ Ltd below.

Remember that variable costs are the costs that vary in a direct relationship with sales.

It is important to recognise that these gross margins are likely to be eroded over time as was shown in chapter 2 and you must show in your profit & loss how you will counter this decline. In many businesses there is likely to be an optimal level of sales that makes maximum use of the staff and other resources. When the business takes the next step in increasing facilities, such as manufacturing capacity, efficiency and gross margins will fall.

When you have established the **gross profit** of the business, you can work on the fixed costs of the business such as management, office costs, insurance, auditing, marketing and depreciation of capital equipment. Do not obscure the picture with too great a breakdown of these fixed costs: group them into relevant areas, eg 'office costs' rather than 'stationery', 'phone' etc, 'power' rather than 'gas', 'electricity' etc. These fixed costs can be determined by you much more easily than the sales and variable costs. As we have seen, much of this is determined by choices that you need to make. Again, bear in mind that these fixed costs are likely to increase in step changes rather than in a straight line.

By deducting the fixed costs from the gross profit, you will produce a profit before interest and tax. You can then deduct these two and provide a **net profit**. In the example of XYZ Ltd on p.138, interest payments have been consolidated into 'bank costs' for the sake of simplicity and tax is shown separately only in the balance sheet which follows (p.141).

XYZ Limited											
Projected profit and loss											
	Jul-08	Aug-08	Sep-08	Oct-08	Nov-08	Dec-08	Q1 2009	Q2 2009	TOTAL 2008–9	2009–10	2010–11
SALES				180,000	360,000	480,000	1,560,000	1,560,000	4,140,000	6,885,000	7,650,000
COST OF SALES (variable costs)											
Raw materials			16,200	64,800	129,600	172,800	561,600	561,600	1,506,600	2,478,600	2,754,000
Packaging			6,300	25,200	50,400	67,200	218,400	218,400	585,900	963,900	1,071,000
Labour			18,000	36,000	63,000	72,000	234,000	234,000	657,000	1,053,000	1,170,000
Distribution costs				3,600	7,200	9,600	31,200	31,200	82,800	137,700	153,000
Power			600	1,800	3,600	4,800	15,600	15,600	42,000	68,850	76,500
TOTAL COST OF SALES			41,100	131,400	253,800	326,400	1,060,800	1,060,800	2,874,300	4,702,050	5,224,500
GROSS PROFIT			-41,100	48,600	106,200	153,600	499,200	499,200	1,265,700	2,182,950	2,425,500
GROSS MARGIN %				27.0%	29.5%	32.0%	32.0%	32.0%	30.6%	31.7%	31.7%
OVERHEADS (fixed costs)											
Rent and rates	7,000	7,000	11,750	10,600	10,600	13,250	34,450	34,450	129,100	137,800	137,800
Insurance	2,400	2,400	3,000	2,400	2,400	3,000	7,800	7,800	31,200	35,100	39,000
Directors' pay		5,000	8,000	10,000	10,000	10,000	30,000	30,000	103,000	120,000	150,000
Office salaries		11,650	25,300	49,940	64,925	49,940	164,805	164,805	531,365	756,660	824,020
Travel	2,400	2,400	3,000	2,400	2,400	3,000	7,800	7,800	31,200	35,100	39,000
Professional fees	2,400	2,400	3,000	3,600	3,600	4,500	11,700	11,700	42,900	52,700	58,500
Misc. costs	1,200	2,100	5,100	11,400	7,215	49,485	89,700	89,700	255,900	403,700	448,500
Bank costs			8,000	3,600	8,000	8,720	22,222	21,581	72,123	65,210	40,098
Depreciation			6,000	12,000	15,600	19,500	50,700	50,700	154,500	225,200	247,200
TOTAL	**15,400**	**32,950**	**73,150**	**105,940**	**124,740**	**161,395**	**419,177**	**418,536**	**1,351,288**	**1,831,470**	**1,984,118**
NET PROFIT/(LOSS)	-15,400	-32,950	-114,250	-57,340	-18,540	-7,795	80,023	80,664	-85,588	351,480	441,382
NET MARGIN %				-31.9%	-5.2%	-1.6%	5.1%	5.2%	-2.1%	5.1%	5.8%
CUM NET PROFIT/(LOSS)	-15,400	-48,350	-162,600	-219,940	-238,480	-246,275	-166,252	-85,588	-85,588	265,892	707,274

ACTION POINT

Prepare a profit & loss forecast showing the various revenue lines that you expect to generate from your business and the corresponding expenditure areas.

Balance sheet

In order to tie the cash flow forecast and the profit & loss forecast together, you need to add a balance sheet forecast.

The balance sheet balances assets and liabilities and will take into account fixed assets such as property and machinery, short-term assets such as cash and debtors (what is owed by customers), short-term liabilities such as creditors (what you owe to suppliers), and long-term liabilities such as bank loans.

In addition, the balance sheet will indicate whether the business is going to have a suitable level of gearing. This means the balance of equity finance provided by shareholders and debt finance provided by banks, for example. In theory, there are several reasons why 'debt is good' and preferable to equity, for example, debt is said to 'make managers get up in the morning', and interest on debt has tax benefits (it can be subtracted from profits when calculating tax whereas dividend payments to shareholders cannot be deducted). Equity returns on capital will also be higher to shareholders where debt replaces equity in a successful business, because the same profit will be spread over fewer shares as the cash has come from a bank rather then additional shareholders. Unfortunately, as many businesses have discovered painfully to their cost, if businesses falter in bad times an excessive amount of debt, which needs to be repaid at set intervals, can cripple a business and cause its insolvency. Setting the correct balance of debt and equity for a business so that returns/rewards are maximised for shareholders but risk is minimised is a vital element of financial modelling. However, due to its complexity, you may choose to assess this in discussion with a financial advisor.

TOP TIPS

There are some software tools available such as Business Plan Pro, Sage's Winforecast and Cashflowwizard, which will ensure that the linking between each forecast and report between the spreadsheets is without errors. Some banks also provide similar software. If you are starting from scratch with a spreadsheet such as MS-Excel, check at all times that the three elements of the financial model (balance sheet, cash flow and profit & loss) are able to work together without errors.

ACTION POINT

Prepare a balance sheet forecast and ensure that it does not conflict with the cash flow and profit & loss forecasts.

ASSUMPTIONS – THE VITAL MISSING LINK

It is a common mistake in business plans for the financial model to follow the wording without any connection between the two sections. It is relatively simple to produce a financial model forecasting the future for the business, showing a rosy future after a challenging start. However, most readers of business plans will be sceptical about such models unless they are accompanied by a robust narrative explaining and defending the assumptions behind the model.

Key questions to make sure you answer are:

- What is the research behind the sales forecast?
- Can you demonstrate that the variable costs are realistic and likely to remain so?
- How can you justify the gross margins both now and in the future? Can you point to competitor analysis?

XYZ Limited								
Projected balance sheets								
	30th Dec 2008			30th Dec 2009			30th Dec 2010	
FIXED ASSETS								
Cost		1,350,000			1,500,000			1,650,000
Depreciation		-154,500			-379,700			-626,900
		1,195,500			1,120,300			1,023,100
CURRENT ASSETS								
Stock	164,000			188,000			212,000	
Debtors	600,000			675,000			750,000	
VAT	46,909			52,255			57,592	
Cash at bank	70,003			247,286			480,644	
	880,912			1,162,541			1,500,236	
CURRENT LIABILITIES								
Trade creditors	318,000			357,750			397,500	
Corporation tax				55,837			110,346	
	318,000			413,587			507,846	
		562,912			748,954			992,390
		1,758,412			1,869,254			2,015,490
Represented by								
SHARE CAPITAL								
Issued shares		1,250,000			1,250,000			1,250,000
PROFIT & LOSS ACCOUNT								
Balance brought forward				-85,588			210,055	
Profit/(loss) for the year	-85,588			295,643			331,036	
		-85,588			210,055			541,091
BANK LOAN		594,000			409,199			224,399
		1,758,412			1,869,254			2,015,490

- What evidence is there for the fixed costs being adequate and appropriate?
- Can you show supplier and customer agreements with agreed terms of business?

This information should all have been covered in your market research and operations planning but needs to be linked to your financial assumptions to back them up.

Raising finance

You need to describe clearly not just how much money you will need by reference to the financial model, but also when it will be needed, for what purposes and in what form. Recognise that money is not always all needed at the start of the plan but needs to be drawn down against milestones in the future. Achieving these milestones will then raise the credibility of the business and reduce the cost of the finance.

Reasons for raising money can include any or all of the following:

- **Suppliers needing payment before receipt of cash from customers.** This shortfall may be addressed best through the factoring of debts or invoice discounting.
- **Seasonal fluctuations in the business.** This is likely to be addressed best with an overdraft facility.
- **Paying for fixed assets such as machinery.** This may be addressed best with asset finance or bank loan.
- **Payment of salaries and other fixed costs before the business is breaking even with enough gross profit to cover the fixed costs.** This is likely to be addressed best with equity finance from shareholders.

TOP TIPS

Your financial forecasts should clearly show how much money you need. Make sure that you can break this down into what you need it for, when and the most appropriate format for external funding.

Valuing the company

One way to value a company for new shareholders when it is currently unprofitable, or even has not started trading is as follows:

- Multiply the net profit that you are projecting for a year in the future, say £500,000 in year 5, by an industry standard (referring to valuations available on similar companies). In the food industry, for example, this might be to multiply by approximately eight for a private business.
- Discount this figure (£4m) by the annual return that investors might expect from a business at the stage yours is at now, say 60% pa or a multiple of 10 after five years.
- This would give a current valuation for the business of £400,000.
- If £250,000 is needed now in order to enable the business to achieve this, the pre-investment value of the business will be £150,000.

The Enterprise Finance Guarantee Scheme

In chapter 1 we looked at raising finance through the Enterprise Finance Guarantee Scheme. This scheme is one of the ways in which you can raise the necessary finance for your business.

EFG is a £1.3bn scheme that supports bank lending, of three months to 10 year maturity, to UK businesses with a turnover of up to £25m who are currently not easily able to access the finance they need. It enables them to secure loans of between £1,000 and £1m through the Government guarantee and is available up to 31 March 2010, although it will hopefully be extended to be applicable for a longer period of time.

The guarantee can be used to support new loans, refinance existing loans, or to convert part or all of an existing overdraft into a loan to release capacity to meet working capital requirements.

The EFG is a joint venture between the Department for Business, Enterprise and Regulatory Reform (BERR) and a number of participating lenders. It is the participating lenders who administer the eligibility criteria and make all commercial decisions regarding borrowing. Once an application has been assessed by the receiving bank and recommended for approval, the loan is then submitted to the Government body only for rubber stamping, with the paperwork typically taking a matter of weeks from start to finish. The Enterprise Finance Guarantee is available now through 23 lenders.

The main features and criteria of the scheme are currently:

- A guarantee to the lender covers 75% of the loan amount, for which the borrower pays a small premium on the outstanding balance of the loan.
- The ability to guarantee loans of up to £1m and with terms of up to 10 years.
- Availability to qualifying UK businesses with an annual turnover of up to £25m.
- Availability to businesses in most sectors and for most business purposes, although there are some restrictions and the standard principles of bank lending, referring to the strength of the proposition and the credibility of the management team, still apply.

Repayment/exit

You should also address the question of how you are going to repay the finance. When will the business be able to afford capital repayments of loans? How will the business return money to shareholders?

In the case of a bank loan, the timing of repayment (as well as the ongoing cost of interest) is likely to be agreed at the time the loan is taken out and needs to be adhered to.

In the case of equity finance, it is not sufficient to adopt the mantra 'Exit by trade sale or IPO (initial public offering or flotation of shares on public stock markets) in three to five years'. First of all, an IPO, if it is available, is often not an exit route but a means to raise funds and make the shares of a private company tradable. Secondly, it is not always possible to sell shares at an IPO because market conditions may not be favourable. A trade sale (sale to another company) or management buy-out (purchase of the shares by the management) are the most likely exit routes for investors in an early-stage company. Therefore, it is helpful to demonstrate that management expectations are aligned with those of shareholders, in that both parties have a plan to sell shares at the same time.

It is also helpful to show that you have considered what sort of company would be interested in buying yours. What elements of your business, as you plan it to grow, will create value for others? Why will a larger company perceive value in your business in the future? Does your growth strategy reflect the likely attraction of your business in the future to the main players in your industry?

It will help to document some of the recent acquisitions of smaller companies by larger companies in your industry, along with the values achieved. You will often find this information in the trade press or financial press. In addition, you could refer to companies in your industry which are likely to find your business attractive to acquire when you have achieved the outcomes laid out in the business plan.

TOP TIPS

It is probably unwise at this stage to propose a valuation for the equity finance that you want to raise, since this will serve only to set an upper limit to such a valuation.

QUICK RECAP

- *Concentrate on the aspects of the financial model that matter:*
  - *Cash, sales forecast, margins, fixed costs.*
  - *Timing of cash payments vs profitability.*
  - *Break-even levels.*
  - *Balance sheet gearing and timing.*
- *Generate a cash flow forecast, a profit & loss forecast and a balance sheet forecast. Make them monthly for the first year and quarterly for years 2 and 3.*
- *Even more importantly, ensure that the assumptions behind the financial model are documented and defensible.*
- *If you are raising finance, do not forget to state how much you need, what it is needed for, when, and in what form.*
- *Explain how and when finance will be repaid.*

CHAPTER 11

Identifying risks and defining actions

This chapter will look at the next stage of your business plan: assessing the risks of your business, and putting together an action plan. Risk is inherent in all businesses, both for management and investors. We will look at the key risks you need to address in a business plan, rather than the everyday risks inherent in a normal business. Once that is done, it is time to look at how you plan to make your plans a reality by assigning key tasks and creating an action plan.

RISKS RELEVANT TO YOUR BUSINESS

In your business plan there is little point in discussing the risks of fire and theft, which you will be insuring for. However, there are some risks which are so great that they will stop a business in its tracks, and a reasonable business plan will show that the management understands whether these risks can be tackled or not. A good business plan will specify how you have addressed such risks.

TOP TIPS

Some commercial risks are normal business risks which can be addressed by normal business means. There is little advantage, for example, in pointing out the obvious fact that if sales fall below expectations you will increase the expenditure on sales and marketing: it probably goes without saying.

One of the biggest risks in an early-stage business is that the key manager (often the founder but perhaps the sales director) is incapacitated or dies. This can be addressed by 'Keyman' life insurance and/or critical illness insurance and the banks or investors will often insist on such cover. The problem can also be addressed by having contingency management plans in such a circumstance. You should also have referred to this in the management section (chapter 9) regarding succession planning in normal times, but a plan for who will run the business in an emergency will show sense and foresight.

Other risks can involve health and safety, especially in food businesses and services to the general public. A bout of listeria or salmonella can result in customers or Government officials insisting on factory or restaurant closure. A contingency plan for this may be as difficult as one for when a fire occurs, but at least if you refer to the risk the reader of the plan will be relieved to know that you understand the problems you might face in the future.

There is also a significant risk which can arise from data loss. Without your computers and the data on them, such as customer details, your business is unlikely to function. Specify the data backup procedures in brief and lay out the risk management policy.

ACTION POINT

Make a list of the three biggest risks that could adversely affect your business and demonstrate how you will mitigate each of these. In this section a SWOT analysis (see below) of the short-term strengths and weaknesses of the business may be useful, along with an analysis of the longer term opportunities and threats to the business. However, a SWOT analysis is not useful or necessary unless it has been carefully considered and leads to conclusions of how to run the business.

SWOT analysis template

Strengths (internal focus) What are the positive aspects of your product/service?	**Weaknesses (internal focus)** What are the negative aspects of your product/service?
Opportunities (external focus) What opportunities can you identify from activity in the world outside your business?	**Threats (external focus)** What threats can you identify from activity in the world outside your business?

In many of these high risk areas, insurance is available albeit at a significant cost. Where it is not available or affordable, the reader of your plan needs to know that you recognise the possibly limitless risks involved.

Risk from technological change can also be devastating. All the issues of competitors introducing new products and technologies described in chapter 7 can be devastating, but you need to be addressing those issues by constant innovation in your own business. Consider again the example of Hewlett-Packard or other companies, where most of the revenues come from products not available a year ago (see chapter 2). Sony's product range also has a similarly limited lifespan, with new products regularly superseding last year's model, creating a constant demand for the next big thing.

Showing that you understand the nature of all risks in your business and having them as much under control as possible will give comfort to the business plan reader that you are not just looking at the day-to-day issues in your business but taking a more long-term view.

SETTING UP AN ACTION PLAN

With the risks addressed you need to start thinking about what comes next. For many purposes a business plan without an action plan would be incomplete. But it is most important to have a plan for action when written for internal purposes, to satisfy your own management team, as opposed to external fundraising purposes.

It is important to allocate tasks to specific people in order to achieve the goals that the business plan has identified. These tasks need to address the full scope of the business plan in terms of all goals and timeframes. It will be a guide for future activity and be a point to refer back to. They need to be realistic in terms of who can complete them, and have milestones against which progress can be monitored.

The best format for this is a spreadsheet with the columns allocated to weeks or months. The rows will be allocated to groups of tasks with headings referring to areas of responsibility, such as Sales & Marketing, Staff, Operations, Finance, Other, each in priority order with a traffic light system of red, yellow and green depending on whether the task is on time or not (see the example for more details on p.152). This will serve as a model for you to refer back to over time and ensure that you are meeting the time requirements of the plan. If not, then the plan will need to be revisited and several tasks may need to be revised.

TOP TIPS

Bear in mind that it is essential to include only tasks to which the SMART principles (see p.48) apply.

ACTION PLAN

		Week 1	Week 2	Week 3	Week 4	Week 5	Week 6	Week 7	Week 8	Week 9	Week 10	Week 11	Week 12	Week 13
		01-Jan	08-Jan	15-Jan	22-Jan	29-Jan	05-Feb	12-Feb	19-Feb	26-Feb	05-Mar	12-Mar	19-Mar	26-Mar
Sales and marketing	Responsibility													
Staff														
Production														
Financial														
Other														

QUICK RECAP

- *Consider the major risks in your business and how you are going to mitigate them.*
- *Remember that normal business risks will be dealt with by normal business practices. Do not overburden the reader with the obvious.*
- *Remember to consider the risks of rapid technological change in your sector.*
- *An action plan is essential to make sure all your goals in the business plan are achieved.*
- *For almost all businesses, an action plan will complement a full business plan by setting realistic milestones and responsibilities which can be monitored over time.*

CHAPTER 12

Executive summary and presentation

This chapter addresses the often misunderstood aspect of the business plan's executive summary as well as the more general presentation of the whole plan.

THE EXECUTIVE SUMMARY

The executive summary is a summary of the rest of the business plan and should be no more than two pages. If it can be covered in one page, so much the better. It is crucial to give a flavour of your business plan and grab the reader's interest but, unfortunately, many summaries frequently let down all the effort put into the plan by not being engaging enough.

You should include the following information, provided that it is relevant, and exclude any unnecessary detail:

- What is the market opportunity?
- What is the value in your product or service?
- What differentiates your offering from other people's?
- Who are the people behind the business?
- How much money (if any) is required, when and in what form?
- How will the investor exit and get a return on their money?

Many people write the summary first, but it is impossible to summarise what you have not yet written. Write it when you have written everything else, but let it appear at the beginning of the document.

Most importantly, it should be written in a different style from the rest of the document. Avoid the temptation to copy and paste sections from the main body of the plan. The summary serves a key purpose which is to excite the reader sufficiently to read the rest of the plan, so it needs to be written with this purpose in mind. Often the reader does not read on beyond the summary because their attention has not been grabbed. Adopting a passionate style is critical and is clearly visible in the opening paragraphs of the following extract.

For another example of a good complete executive summary see appendix 2.

EXAMPLE

Sample Executive Summary

To join the C Club you have simply to believe in and wish to recapture the style and glamour of the glorious period between 1920 and 1960. The Club aims to be the most sought after membership in the world by invigorating and pushing its members towards a more fulfilled life. The Club will give access to shared experience, open doors which might otherwise be shut and offer up a camaraderie which lifts the experience from the quotidian to the extraordinary.

The C Club will have a spirit not seen since the 1920s and 1960s, where members can live a little of the life lived by Jim Clark and Stirling Moss, the Rat Pack, James Dean and Hemingway. It is about a set of values which members will develop with the Club. The Club seeks a maximum membership of 1,000, high net worth individuals in phase 1 of its life. These people have few conflicts for their money and, by organising great events which are beautiful in style and provide access to a range of high-value, limited edition luxury goods, the Club will make a convincing case for their money and time.

Despite the Club's feeling of mutuality, it will be a money-making organisation seeking to provide a return for investors. Run by Peter Adams, a highly successful entrepreneur with a small, highly qualified board, the club also has a number of well-connected Ambassadors who will promote the Club's interests worldwide. The Club will seek exit by private sale within 10 years.

The Club will have a number of spiritual homes rather than one fixed headquarters. It will exist through vivid experiences of single and multi-day events divided into, initially, seven broad themes, Motor Racing and Touring, Goodwood Experience, Alpine Experience, Kenya and Cuba Experiences, Debrett's City Challenge and Short Events in London. The Club will start its life with Motor Racing and Short Events. The Motor Racing section will offer seasonal ownership, track days, a Le Mans pilgrimage, a route to a racing licence and European Grand Touring. Events will be subsidised by Sponsors. Members will be able to access luxury brands and specialist Kit as well as have the opportunity to buy special edition New Vintage cars refined by the Club designer Studio-C.

TOP TIPS

Ask independent people to read the summary and assess its impact. Are they excited by what is being offered? If not, you probably need to change the style.

The summary should whet the reader's appetite, excite them and invite them to ask questions which will be answered in the main plan. It does not have to cover every angle.

If you are using the plan as a tool to raise equity finance, do not feel obliged to suggest a deal or a valuation. This will serve only to cap the potential value; however, when you start to talk to potential investors you should have some idea of the business' current value. This may be by reference to similar businesses or to a multiple of projected profits, but this preparation will enable you to defend your position robustly.

STYLE AND PRESENTATION

Now that you have put the content of the plan together consider how attractive you might make its presentation for the reader. There are now so many sufficiently low-cost software tools in existence, including MS-Word and MS-Excel, that it is unacceptable for a business plan to look anything other than professional.

A standard business plan will be in A4 format bound on the long edge. However, this may not be the right format. Good plans for internal purposes can come in the form of a poster, which can be put up on the reception wall. MS-Powerpoint may be a more powerful format than MS-Word. Consider the purpose of your business plan and who is your target audience. Whatever the case, a clear, readable font and typeface with simple bold layout and contents page are important. Also, adding some colour (product photos etc) will make the plan a more enjoyable reading experience.

Twenty pages of text in 12-point font should be sufficient for any plan to achieve its objectives. Beyond that the reader is likely to lose attention, and you will not have demonstrated that you understand the business clearly enough. Keep technical information out of the main body of the plan and in appendices but refer to it in the main plan. You might consider bullet points in the margins of the plan summarising the key points of each section, making the reader's task quicker and easier.

As indicated in the financial section in chapter 9, the standard financial model will then add pages as follows: 3 years of profit & loss, cash flow and balance sheet projections, monthly for the first year and quarterly for years 2 and 3. A sensitivity analysis may add a final touch.

Follow the chapters in this book and you will have the structure and content that you need to be set for success. These specific headings may work for you!

- Executive Summary
- Background
- Product/Service
- Market
- Route to market
- Competition
- Operations
- Management
- Financial assumptions and forecasts
- Risks
- Actions

QUICK RECAP

- *An executive summary is the first thing people will read so it needs to excite them and leave them wanting to hear more.*
- *It should summarise the rest of the business plan but be written in quite a different style.*
- *Poor presentation of a business plan is unnecessary and detrimental to the efforts put into the content.*
- *Take care to make the plan easy to read and attractive, short enough to keep the reader's attention but long enough to cover the key points.*
- *Technical information can be added in appendices.*
- *Think carefully about the presentation and style of your business plan – make sure you use the best format for your plan.*

CHAPTER 13

Quickstart guide: summary of key points

CHAPTER 1: THE PURPOSE OF A BUSINESS PLAN

- Work out why you are writing the business plan – is it for the management team or do you need to raise finance?
- If you are looking to raise finance decide on the potential of your business and its immediate capacity to generate cash to help you understand the best route for your business.
- Determine what different audiences will want to read about.
  - Are they a bank that is concerned about security and cash flow?
  - Are they investors who will want explosive growth in the value of their shares and a clearly identifiable way for them to get their money out of your business in three to five years time?
  - Are they existing or future members of the company who you will want to be inspired to work with and for you?
  - Are they interested in buying the business, and so will want to know why you are selling it?
- Work out how you are going to demonstrate that your business can meet their needs.
- Identify your audience – do you have more than one audience type?
- Amend your initial business plan to suit the needs of an additional audience.
- Show your passion to inspire the readers of your business plan with your vision.

CHAPTER 2: TESTING YOUR IDEA

- Before writing your plan you need to assess your business idea rigorously.
- Does the opportunity match your experience, skills and interests?
- Can you recruit and lead the team needed to exploit the opportunity?
- What resources have you got that others are missing?
- Is the timing of the opportunity right?
- Does the opportunity constitute a scalable (and saleable) business?
- Does the opportunity offer good margin potential?
- Are you developing an opportunity or simply an idea?
- What value are you offering to your customers?
- What innovation are you planning in your business now and in the future?
- Only once you have done your groundwork are you ready to move on to start thinking about your business plan.

CHAPTER 3: TIMING, VISION AND BACKGROUND

- The business plan should be regarded as a document that you revisit regularly.
- Do not treat the plan as a one-off necessary burden.
- Do not write the plan only at start-up and when you need it for the bank.
- Write the plan in good times when the future looks rosy so that you are in a strong position to tackle everything that comes your way, rather than be forced to negotiate and compromise when everything is stacked up against you.

- Create and agree on your long-term vision for the business as clearly as possible and then write your business plan to target this long-term vision.
- Understand that there may be several ways to progress from where you are now to attaining your vision. Consider the many different business models that can deliver your vision and then decide which is the most effective means of reaching your desired destination.
- Once you have articulated your vision, explain where the business is now. You will then need to show only how you are going to get from where you are now to where you want to go.

CHAPTER 4: DESCRIBING YOUR PRODUCT OR SERVICE

- Describe your product or service in simple layman's language.
- Set it in the context of the market opportunity that you have identified.
- Do not make this section any longer than it needs to be – this is not a sales brochure.
- Concentrate on the benefits of the product or service to the customer, not on the features.

CHAPTER 5: IDENTIFY YOUR MARKET

- Determine the size of the market starting with the first customer.
- Spend time and, if necessary, money on primary consumer market research.
- Do not work backwards from unsuitable desktop research.
- Take care in defining your market. Your business is likely to be in a relatively small niche of a much larger market.

- Segment the overall market starting with the group of customers which is most attractive to your business.
- Explain why you have identified the market as you have by describing how other providers make money in the market and what they have missed.
- Focus on dominating your chosen niche and the fluctuations of the wider economy through boom and bust will be less important.

CHAPTER 6: ROUTE TO MARKET: PROMOTION, SALES AND DISTRIBUTION

- Consider the many alternative routes to market which are open to your business, starting with the concept of a virtual business.
- Is it appropriate to build your own brand or can you hide behind an established one?
- Alternatives will need to be addressed in each of the three areas of promotion, sales and distribution.
- Balance the costs of building your own resources against using other people's resources.
- Balance the risk of using other people's resources against the strength of keeping a grip on the customer in the business.

CHAPTER 7: COMPETITION

- Don't just address the existing direct competition.
- Consider indirect competition. Think from the customer's point of view and not yours.
- Consider substitute competition. What alternative ways does the customer have to meet their needs?
- Consider future changes to the competitive landscape both because of your planned actions and because of other changes, eg in technology.

CHAPTER 8: OPERATIONS

- Consider all the different options that your business may have in its operations.
- Establish whether it needs to have any fixed infrastructure or whether it can operate virtually.
- Ask yourself whether it needs its own manufacturing capacity or property. If so, what changes will need to be made in the future as volumes increase, and when?
- Explain what methods you have developed to excel at executing the operations.
- Do not forget that great customer service can make the difference between success and failure.

CHAPTER 9: MANAGEMENT

- The management section is the most important part of the business plan. Give it the focus that it needs.
- Consider not only the current management team but also future requirements and how the relevant people are going to be recruited.
- Ensure that the management skills are demonstrated in other appropriate places throughout the plan.
- Make reference not just to the senior managers but also to key staff and the Board, including non-executive directors.
- Establish the future role of the CEO/Founder and when it would be right for him/her to take a back seat in favour of a professional manager.

CHAPTER 10: FINANCIAL ASSUMPTIONS AND INFORMATION

- Concentrate on the aspects of the financial model that matter:
  - Cash, sales forecast, margins, fixed costs.
  - Timing of cash payments vs profitability.
  - Break-even levels.
  - Balance sheet gearing and timing.
- Generate a cash flow forecast, a profit & loss forecast and a balance sheet forecast. Make them monthly for the first year and quarterly for years 2 and 3.
- Even more importantly, ensure that the assumptions behind the financial model are documented and defensible.
- If you are raising finance, do not forget to state how much you need, what it is needed for, when, and in what form.
- Explain how and when finance will be repaid.

CHAPTER 11: IDENTIFYING RISKS AND DEFINING ACTIONS

- Consider the major risks in your business and how you are going to mitigate them.
- Remember that normal business risks will be dealt with by normal business practices. Do not overburden the reader with the obvious.
- Remember to consider the risks of rapid technological change in your sector.
- An action plan is essential to make sure all your goals in the business plan are achieved.
- For almost all businesses, an action plan will complement a full business plan by setting realistic milestones and responsibilities which can be monitored over time.

CHAPTER 12: EXECUTIVE SUMMARY AND PRESENTATION

- An executive summary is the first thing people will read so it needs to excite them and leave them wanting to hear more.
- It should summarise the rest of the business plan but be written in quite a different style.
- Poor presentation of a business plan is unnecessary and detrimental to the efforts put into the content.
- Take care to make the plan easy to read and attractive, short enough to keep the reader's attention but long enough to cover the key points.
- Technical information can be added in appendices.
- Think carefully about the presentation and style of your business plan; make sure you use the best format for your plan.

CHAPTER 14

Troubleshooting

Q: I am starting my business, and I am using my own money to launch the business. Do I need a business plan at all?

A: Yes, almost certainly you do need a business plan, although you need to work out who you are writing it for and why.

There are many reasons for writing a business plan. One of the key reasons is to develop a strategic road map for the long term and an action plan for the short-term. Without a business plan you are likely to default to fire fighting in the business and forget your vision and strategy. Above all, a comprehensive business plan will highlight the weaknesses in future funding, management etc. You will be able to use the business plan as a basis for discussion with colleagues and managers. You will be able to refer back to the business plan in the future. Above all, it is a means of testing alternative business models and bringing discipline to your thinking about the business.

Q: My friends tell me that my business idea is great. Do I need to do any market research?

A: A professional approach to market research will underpin a business plan and prove to be of real value. This can be a combination of desktop research and primary consumer market research. Of the two, the primary consumer market research is the most important. If you rely on friends and family for their opinions to determine whether you should launch new products and services your data will be inappropriate and misleading. In addition, it will be much more difficult to raise finance from sceptical investors.

The market research needs to involve a carefully tailored set of questions so that you can compile data that is meaningful in the business plan. Remember why you are doing it, for example to validate sales forecasts. Employing the services of a professional research firm may be money well spent.

Q: Anyone is a potential buyer of my service. Does my business have global reach?

A: Your business may have global potential, but thinking about the business in these terms is a common trap when developing a business plan. Even if it is true that anyone might want what you have to sell, you will find it much easier to build your business by focusing on well-defined segments of the population that want your products most.

By increasing your market from the smallest position rather than approaching the largest position from the start, you will understand your customers' needs and how to meet those needs. It will make the task of reaching the widest possible audience practical. It is up to you to decide how to select the most sensible segments of the market based on sound market research.

Q: I have a great website. Is this sufficient to generate sales for my business?

A: Having a website is like having a sales brochure. It is useless unless you can ensure that plenty of people know about it and have access to it. Therefore, you need to concentrate on how you might achieve this without it costing a prohibitive amount. Search engine optimisation (improving your position in search engine listings) and viral marketing (by word-of-mouth through social sites such as Facebook) may help, but it is most likely that your website will be just one of the means of drawing attention to your business: you will also need direct sales channels or distributors.

A great website is becoming an essential tool for any business. You should consider whether it is just a means of marketing your products and services or whether you can use new technology such as video webinars to reach customers more effectively. If you are going to use the website as a platform for sales, ensure that the payment process is simple and there is a means of contacting you for help. (See *Successful Websites* (Crimson Publishing, 2009) for more information on this.)

Q: My product is unique. Why do I need to identify competitors?

A: Believing that your product is unique is likely to be misguided. You need to look widely at what options your prospective customers have when making their buying decisions. You need to look at various, different types of competitor: direct competitors (those selling the same as you in the same way), indirect competitors (those selling something that meets your customers' needs in a different way from you, for example by a different means of distribution), and substitute competitors (those taking your customers' budgets but not selling what you are selling). You also need to think about how the marketplace will change over time when new competitors notice the success that you are having. The nature of competition is complex, but you will understand it better if you view it from your customers' position rather than your own.

Q: I am worried about building up the permanent infrastructure of my business. How can I build the business without any fixed costs?

A: This is one of the frequent dilemmas in a business plan – balancing the essentally fixed costs of building your own operation with the control that they might bring. There are many ways to build a business without creating your own infrastructure:

including freelance employees, outsourcing manfacturing, and franchising. Each of these models has pros and cons. Long-term employment contracts, long leases on property and internally trained salesforces all give security but also prevent rapid movement in changed circumstances. Serviced offices may meet your unknown future needs better than a long lease with no break clause. On the other hand, security of tenure in a retail unit may be essential in ensuring the best High Street location. Outsourcing removes many of the fixed costs generally associated with business and enables you to focus on the aspect of your business in which your expertise lies. However, other companies may not have the passion for your products and services that you have.

Q: I have run a business before and can cover all aspects of management. Do I need a team of managers?

A: If you plan to build your business, the needs of the business will be very different in three years' time from what they are now. The business plan can help you to think about who you will need to recruit in the future. One of the best ways to enable a business to grow is to hire the best possible people to manage each of the core functions, especially sales, finance, and operations. You may find that you are the best person to lead the company but not the best in all of these line functions. You may even discover that you can find someone better than you to run the whole company while you excel in your chosen field of management. Delegation by you to others will free up your time to expand the business by whatever means are best.

You will also find that there is less risk inherent for investors in a team of managers than there is in an individual entrepreneur. Raising finance will be very difficult without a credible team of managers who have complementary skills.

Q: I know from my financial forecasts that I need £200,000 to expand my business. Where do I find it?

A: This question in reality combines several questions.

First of all, what form should the finance take? Do you need a short-term overdraft facility because of the business cycle, for example to finance high stocks at certain seasons of the year? Do you need an invoice discounting facility to cope with rapid growth in sales on credit? Do you need asset financing to pay for machinery? In these cases, you would probably be most sensible to talk to banks and finance companies. If the finance required is longer term in order to pay for the start-up losses that you will incur before you have critical mass and profitability, then equity finance is probably more suitable, possibly in combination with bank debt under The Enterprise Finance Guarantee Scheme.

If you find that you need equity finance, £200,000 is most likely to come from business angels, unless you have wealthy friends and family. These angels are likely to be found either through word-of-mouth referral or through the British Business Angels Association (www.bbaa.org.uk) or Business Plan Services' BPS Connect service (http://www.bizplans.co.uk/bps_connect/bps_connect.asp).

APPENDIX 1

Executive summary example

WORLDWIDE HEALTHCARE DEVICES

INTRODUCTION

Worldwide Healthcare Devices Mexico SA de CV (legally constituted in Mexico in September 2007) has been charged with conducting the medical tests and commercialisation of an invention patented by US-based Worldwide Healthcare Devices LLC, which was founded in August 2006. Worldwide Healthcare Devices LLC (WHD) is the proprietor of the patents for the invention **Intra-gastro Balloon Device** (IBD) that will be used to treat severe and morbid obesity as an alternative to current surgical practice but with the same level of efficiency, at much lower cost and with far fewer medical risks.

SIZE OF THE MARKET AND ITS GROWTH POTENTIAL AND REVENUE STREAMS

Current demographic figures show that in many countries obesity is already a significant public health problem. Obesity is considered to be the second leading cause of preventable death (Source: American Obesity Association). It is calculated that, worldwide, there are some 1.6 billion people who are overweight, of whom more than 400 million are classified as obese (Source: World Health Organisation (WHO) 2005). Furthermore, these figures are set to dramatically rise according to WHO which projects that, by 2015, approximately 2.3 billion adults will be overweight and more than 700 million of them will be obese. According to the International Obesity Task Force (IOTF) approximately half of the population in Europe is already overweight and 20% of these people are classified as being obese. In 2002 the prevalence of morbid obesity in the US was 1.8% which creates a massive market of 7 million people in the US alone. WHD is targeting a 5% share of the US market which equates to sales of 360,000 devices and an income of $360m by year five of operation. Whilst obesity is a problem that is growing at a phenomenal rate in most wealthy nations of the world, further growth should be expected as developing nations prosper and their middle classes grow, extending WHD's potential market to include India, China etc.

Morbid obesity can be treated either medically (with drugs) or surgically (bariatric surgery). Studies have shown that a surgical option is the most effective way to achieve and maintain weight loss, significantly reducing major co-morbidities. Currently the treatment of choice for the morbidly obese is major bariatric surgery to restrict the amount of food that can be absorbed.

Over the last 10 years significant annual increases in the performance of weight loss procedures in the United States has been noted, reaching more than 175,000 cases in 2005 (up from 140,000 surgeries in 2004). It is estimated that the number of surgeries worldwide for treatment of obesity is approximately 1 million with significant annual growth. It has been estimated that the cost of treating obesity in the United States alone was approximately $117bn, of which $61bn is related to direct medical costs. Current surgical techniques cost in the order of $30,000 per patient. The number of bariatric surgeries in the United States is projected to reach approximately 400,000 annually by 2010 (JP Morgan Analyst Report, October 2005, Monitor Group).

The stapling or bypass surgery involves long hospital stays, significant additional health risks and is not suitable for many patients. Against this backdrop an exciting opportunity undoubtedly exists to introduce a new method of treatment that is less costly, carries fewer risks and is proven to deliver at least similar results.

UNIQUE FEATURES AND ROUTE TO MARKET

The IBD device is a simple prosthetic designed to restrict a person's food intake. The device can be implanted with minor surgery allowing the patient to leave hospital on the same day, thus reducing the costs associated with major surgery and a prolonged hospital stay. The procedure is minimally invasive and thus reduces the chance of complications that can follow from major surgery. The procedure can be temporary or permanent as the balloons can be replaced. Other surgical interventions are permanent. It should be noted that the IBD device could also be used in obese patients and not just those with morbid obesity. This would have the effect of radically increasing the possible market for the product. Other bariatric surgeries are not considered suitable for this group of patients owing to the cost and health risk factors involved. The IBD device overcomes these obstacles and fears.

The IBD device and procedure will represent a direct and fierce competitor to the current major bariatric surgical treatments. The principal line of business will be the marketing and distribution of the IBD device to medical specialists for the treatment of patients with morbid and minor obesity in Mexico, the USA, the UK and Continental Europe where patents are now granted. The surgical procedures involved are straightforward for immediate implementation without the need for any on-site support.

BUSINESS VALUE PROPOSITION

The essential value proposition is that the IBD is:

- A cheaper procedure, based on the device costing $1,200 and the total procedure costing $5,000, compared with other bariatric surgical procedures that typically cost $30,000.
- Quicker and less invasive with fewer surgical complications, available to most patients even those with co-morbidities.
- Has (at least) equal outcomes to procedures with which it will therefore be able to compete most favourably.

KEY MANAGEMENT TEAM

Worldwide Healthcare Devices is a family company set up in 2007. The Chief Executive is Carlos Demetrez MD who has 30 years' experience of treatment of patients with gastric problems and obesity. The Chief Commercial/Financial Officer is Pablo Santodar who has a number of years of senior experience with UBS in Switzerland and London. The Chief Technical Officer will be Lorena Gabon. Collectively, the team represent a cohesive group with both sector and functional expertise across a wide range of disciplines. Additional expertise will be brought into the venture to support marketing and PR activity although this will be focussed on the niche medical market.

HEADLINE FINANCIALS

In order to commence production and distribution a period of field testing is required. It is the intention to complete 25 cases by April 2009 at a cost of $10,000 per head. Once a successful track record has been established global marketing and distribution will commence in mid 2009. Worldwide Healthcare Devices therefore seeks an investment of $375,000 to complete the trials phase.

In the first year, following completion of the pilot study (2009), sales will commence in Mexico with a total revenue generation of $46,000. It is anticipated that the Mexican equivalent of FDA approval will be easily obtained on the basis of the results from 40–50 patients. Furthermore, Lorena Gabon is currently employed to prepare cases for approval by the Mexican authorities by medical firms seeking approval in Mexico, so the system and people involved are known well to her.

In the second year sales growth will accelerate in Mexico to generate revenues of $660,000. The aggressive sales growth targeted in the business plan will be greatly facilitated owing to the many personal relationships in the medical and hospital fraternity that both Dr Demetrez and Lorena Gabon currently have. The increasing sales and growing evidence base will generate the higher volume of cases that will be required as evidence by the US FDA before they will grant a license for the product. The permissions to sell in the US and Europe will be progressively sought during the first and second years of operation of the business.

It is anticipated that approval in Europe will be easier to achieve owing to the presence of a similar competitor product already approved. In year three sales will commence in the US and by year end $6.1m revenue is forecast, rising to $100m in year five (2013). Break-even occurs in April 2011 with very rapidly increasing positive cash flows thereafter. By the end of year five, net cash flow is $120m.

APPENDIX 2

The art of raising finance from business angels

If you intend to write a business plan for the purposes of raising finance rather than for internal planning purposes or a personal strategic road map, bear in mind a few thoughts about what your potential investor will want to read.

We have already established earlier in the book the difference between a debt provider and an equity investor. The former is interested in security and cash flow to service the debt whereas the latter is interested in explosive capital growth. Both groups will have numerous alternative plans to read, and so the way that the plan is constructed in order to meet their needs is important if you want to reach the top of their pile.

There is much information available about the generic nature of angel investors. In fact, all angels have different experiences and methods of operating. So, it may be worth exploring the angel market before you write the plan to understand which particular group you might appeal to and why. Some factors are likely to be present in most angels.

Equity investors (angels) are principally interested in whether you really have identified a huge potential market opportunity and, if so, how you are going to supply it in preference to your competitors. Next, they want to know whether you (as the founding entrepreneur) have the character to adapt to changing circumstances and also how well your team can work together to deliver the solution to the market needs. Everyone knows that your business plan will not reflect reality throughout the years that it is forecasting: the good management team will spot market changes early enough to exploit them. Thirdly, the investor will want to know that you understand the importance of return on capital (for all shareholders) and exit from the business. Finally, what do you want to receive from the angel in terms of experience, contacts etc, which will enable your business to make most rapid progress?

These points have deliberately been kept short, but they capture the essence of what an angel wants to see clearly and succinctly.

Business plans too rarely understand what the investor wants to see and indeed what they do not need to see. Raising money is not a science: it is an art, but that art must be based on a clear understanding of what matters.

APPENDIX 3

Case studies: the good, the bad and the ugly

You may well have little experience of investors, and so it will come as a surprise that many investors have a lot of experience of entrepreneurs. Here are a few entrepreneur character types that investors are wary of. If you fall into one of these groups you may want to reconsider your management style!

THE ETERNAL OPTIMIST

Entrepreneurs, and salesmen more generally, tend to fall into two camps – the optimists and the pessimists. Whichever camp they fall into, they tend to stay there. Investors understand these traits. Therefore, when you produce a financial forecast in the business plan, ensure that you can support it with realistic data; otherwise it will be used as evidence against you in the future. If circumstances beyond your control change it is reasonable to expect the forecasts to change, but all too often forecasts change because of sloppy and over-optimistic assumptions. Of course, this needs to be balanced with the need for growth forecasts to be ambitious enough to support the investor's expectations for value growth.

Nephelococcus
The eternal optimist

THE PROPRIETOR / CONTROL FREAK

Many entrepreneurs have an issue with ownership of their business. To their mind 100% of a small pot is considered to be worth more than 70% of a large pot. This is unfortunate, not least in its erroneous mathematics. If you are going to invite minority investors into the business, understand that they will be owners of a proportion of the business, entitled to information and other rights. They may want to participate in regular meaningful Board meetings. Life will not be the same as when you were responsible only to yourself. Demonstrate in the business plan that you are happy to embrace this new culture.

Lupus Solus
The Proprietor/control freak

THE KNOW-IT-ALL

Angels can add far more value than money to a business. This value can make an apparently unattractive investment deal very worthwhile, and beyond what you could achieve in any other way. Analyse what benefits you want from your investors, specify them in the business plan and then it is much more likely that your needs will be met by the appropriate incoming investors.

THE KNACKERED ONE – OUT-OF-YOUR DEPTH

Entrepreneurs generally wait far too long before seeking finance. Prepare your business plan well ahead of when you might need the finance. Analyse yourself to ensure that you are still the right person to be running what might otherwise be a great business. If in doubt, ask your management team, and be prepared to act to bring in someone with the experience and skills to take the business to the next level. Perhaps you need to raise more money than you thought in order to finance a new Chief Executive?

Anser Claudus *The Knackered one* **and his cousin** **Mergus Submersus** *Out of his depth*

THE TECHNOLOGIST

Some entrepreneurs, mainly first class scientists, still believe that if you invent what you believe to be the greatest product, the world will beat a path to your door. This has never been, and is unlikely ever to be the case. Make sure that the business plan reflects in-depth research on the market demand for your product or service.

Homo Technologicus
The technology man

THE LIFESTYLE MERCHANT

Understand that the investor will have very different criteria for judging the success of your business from you. The investor is not likely to be making a living from the business or even to be paid a dividend. Therefore, ensure that your financial drawings from the business are modest and reflective of the success of the business. The investor does not want to put money into the business just so that you can extract it.

Porcus Porsche
The lifestyle merchant

THE NON-REPORTING ENTREPRENEUR

Legal agreements matter. Agreements between shareholders, with suppliers and customers and employees all matter, especially when relationships go wrong. Put an appendix in the business plan showing that all these documents exist even if the full details are not included. Financial reporting is also vital when external investors become involved. State how often and in what form management reports are prepared.

Ostrica Innumeratus
The non-finance man

THE PLANNER

Remember that business planning is a real weapon in your armoury towards achieving successful management of the business. However, do not forget that it is very time consuming and you still need to run the business. An action plan in the business plan will show when you are going to stop planning and start executing the many critical tasks that will take your business forward to where it needs to be.

Canis Occupatus
The planner

THE GOLD MINE

If you have navigated these many challenges and written a succinct clear business plan, you will have travelled a very long way towards your goal of raising finance, and you may find that you are able to emulate those successful entrepreneurs who have struck gold in their business. At least you now have the tools to start digging.

Avis Rarissima
The lesser-spotted goldmine

APPENDIX 4

Useful links

GENERAL HELP

- Association of British Insurers
  www.abi.org.uk
  Tel: 020 7600 3333

- British Bankers' Association
  www.bba.org.uk
  Tel: 020 7216 8800

- British Standards Institution
  www.bsi-global.com
  Tel: 020 8996 9001

- Business Link
  www.businesslink.gov.uk
  Tel: 0845 600 9006
  Business Link is a free business advice and support service, available online and through local advisers.

- BVCA British Venture Capital Association
  www.bvca.co.uk
  Tel: 020 7025 2950

- Companies House
  www.companieshouse.gov.uk
  Tel: 0303 123 4500

- Department for Business, Enterprise and Regulatory Reform
  www.berr.gov.uk
  Tel: 020 7215 5000

- HM Revenue and Customs
  www.hmrc.gov.uk

- Law Society
  www.lawsociety.org.uk
  Tel: 020 7242 1222

- Patent Office/Trade Marks Registry
  www.ipo.gov.uk
  Tel: 0845 950 0505

- Professional Contractors Group
  www.pcg.org.uk
  Tel: 0845 125 9899

- The British Chambers of Commerce
  www.britishchambers.org.uk
  Tel: 020 7654 5800

- The Chartered Institute of Patent Agents
  www.cipa.org.uk
  Tel: 020 7405 9450

- London Business School
  www.london.edu

- Foundation for Entrepreneurial Management
  www.london.edu/entrepreneurship.html

- Sussex Place Ventures
  www.spventures.co.uk

FUNDING

- Angel News
  www.angelnews.co.uk
  Tel: 01275 333 443
  Angel News is the commercial news service for angel early-stage funded companies. Angel News is a free focused service for all companies that have been funded by business angels or venture capitalists.

- British Business Angels Association
  www.bbaa.org.uk
  Tel: 0207 089 2305
  The British Business Angels Association (BBAA) is the national trade association for the UK's Business Angel Networks and the early-stage investment market and is backed by the Department for Business, Enterprise and Regulatory Reform (BERR).

- J4B
  www.j4b.co.uk
  Comprehensive and easy to use grants information database.

- London Business Angels
  www.lbangels.co.uk
  Tel: 0207 089 2303
  For the last 25 years London Business Angels has been facilitating investment into early-stage businesses within the UK.

- NESTA
  www.nesta.org.uk
  The National Endowment for Science, Technology and the Arts supports and promotes talent, innovation and creativity through funding and mentoring.

- one London Ltd
  www.gle.co.uk/onelondon
  A subsidiary of Greater London Enterprise Limited that provides business loans, support and private investment to the London community.

- Oxford Innovation Ltd
  www.oxin.co.uk
  Oxford Innovation works in a variety of ways to assist the commercial exploitation and development of innovative science and technology.

MARKET RESEARCH

- Annual Abstract of Statistics
  www.statistics.gov.uk

- Aslib (the Association for Information)
  www.aslib.co.uk
  Can provide list of specialist business libraries in the UK.

- British Library
  www.bl.uk
  Tel: 0870 444 1500
  The Business & IP Centre, at the British Library in London, has extensive information and assistance resources available to innovators and entrepreneurs.

- Datamonitor
  www.datamonitor.com
  Global data collection and in-depth analysis across any industry.

- Economist Intelligence Unit
  www.store.eiu.com
  Country specific global business analysis.

- Euromonitor
  www.euromonitor.com
  A leading provider of global market information with 30 years of research experience.

- Ipsos MORI
  www.ipsos-mori.com

- Key Note Ltd
  www.keynote.co.uk

- Mintel
  www.mintel.com
  Consumer market research.

- Survey Monkey
  www.surveymonkey.com
  Create professional online surveys quickly and easily.

- The Market Research Society
  www.marketresearch.org.uk

- Verdict
  www.verdict.co.uk
  Retail research specialists.

BUSINESS SUPPORT SERVICES

- Startups
  Startups.co.uk is the UK's leading website for anyone considering starting or running a small business providing information and advice as well as a start-up business community, a lively forum, entrepreneur video and podcasts and free business networking events and webinars.

- Growing Business
  www.growingbusiness.co.uk
  Growing Business is the UK's most popular magazine for entrepreneurs. Now, not only in print, the website boasts live interviews with the most sought after names in business as well as practical, useable advice to help your business grow.

- Beermat
  Beermat.biz is the official website of Mike Southon and Chris West, 'The Beermat Entrepreneurs'. Beermat.biz provides free networking events, sales training, Beermat Radio business podcasts, freebies and more to help you build a great business.

- Businessmax
  Provides tools and services to prepare vital legal paperwork, covering HR & Employment, Health & Safety, Debt Recovery, Contracts & Letters.

- Business Plan Services
  www.bizplans.co.uk
  Tel: 0845 057 4065
  Business Plan Services is the definitive resource for business planning in the UK.

- Connect London
  www.connectlondon.org
  Tel: 020 8545 2875
  Connect London assists technology and high growth potential businesses by helping them to obtain funding and connecting them to mentors, training, academic support, business service suppliers and professional firms as well as a network of businesses and women with similar aspirations.

- IP21
  www.ip21.co.uk
  Tel: 020 7645 8250
  IP21 offers the full range of services expected from a leading patent and trademark firm, plus additional commercial and design services.
- ivegotanidea
  www.ivegotanidea.co.uk
  Tel: 0845 057 4065
  Pulling together six of the best free and special offers for a full range of support services to help get a business idea off the ground.

- RM2
  www.rm2.co.uk
  The RM2 Partnership designs, implements and administers share ownership schemes, share option schemes, share purchase arrangements and other incentive solutions.

- Striding Out
  www.stridingout.co.uk
  Striding Out is a pioneering support network for young people, aged 18–30, with enterprising ambitions.

- The Telegraph Business Club
  www.telegraphbusinessclub.co.uk

Index